SING-ALONG WITH
EASY FINGERPIC
GUITAR
ACCOMPANIMENT

C000156419

ISBN 978-1-4584-4136-2

HAL•LEONARD®
CORPORATION
7777 W. BLUEMOUND RD. P.O. BOX 13819 MILWAUKEE, WI 53213

For all works contained herein:
Unauthorized copying, arranging, adapting, recording, Internet posting, public performance,
or other distribution of the printed or recorded music in this publication is an infringement of copyright.
Infringers are liable under the law.

Visit Hal Leonard Online at
www.halleonard.com

CONTENTS

Against All Odds
(Take a Look at Me Now)
from AGAINST ALL ODDS
Words and Music by Phil Collins

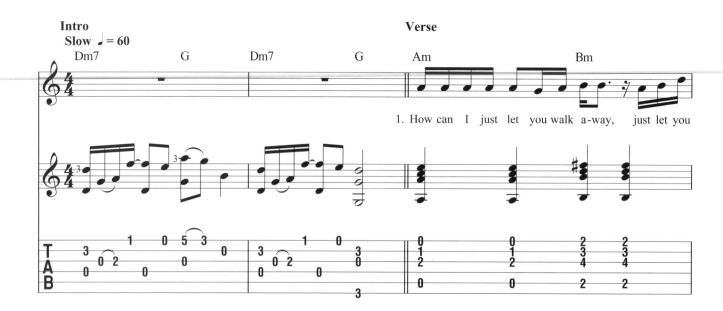

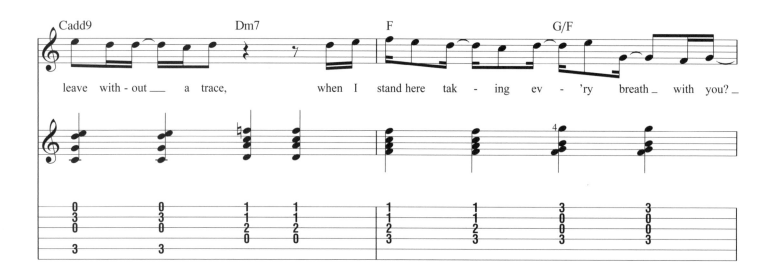

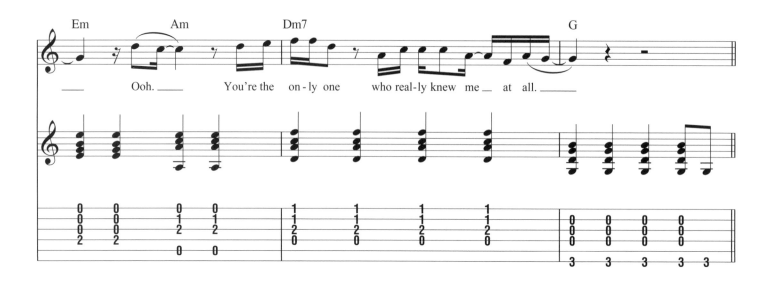

© 1984 IMAGEM MUSIC, PHILIP COLLINS LTD. and EMI GOLDEN TORCH MUSIC CORP.
Exclusive Print Rights for EMI GOLDEN TORCH MUSIC CORP. Administered by ALFRED MUSIC PUBLISHING CO.
All Rights Reserved   International Copyright Secured   Used by Permission

Verse

2. How can you just walk a - way from me, when all I can do is watch you leave? 'Cause we've
wish I could just make you turn a - round, turn a - round and see me cry. There's so

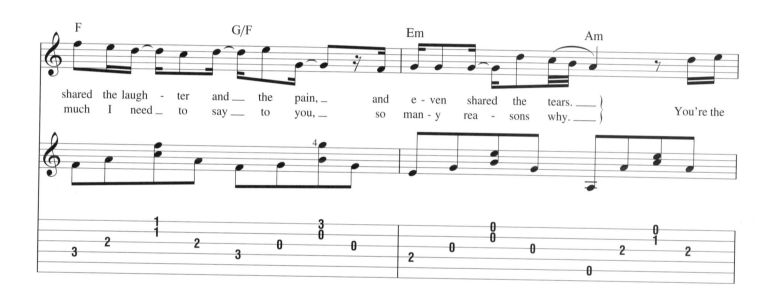

shared the laugh - ter and the pain, and e - ven shared the tears. You're the
much I need to say to you, so man - y rea - sons why.

on - ly one who real - ly knew me at all. So take a look at me now,

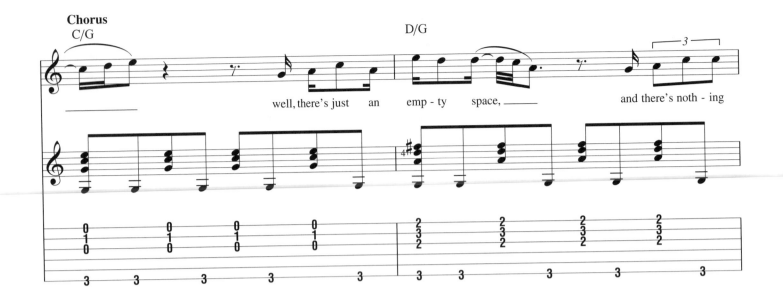

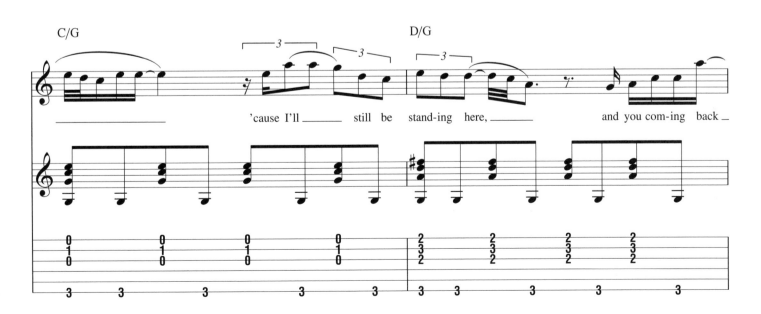

_____ to me _____ is a - gainst _ all odds, _ it's the chance I've got - ta take. _____

Outro

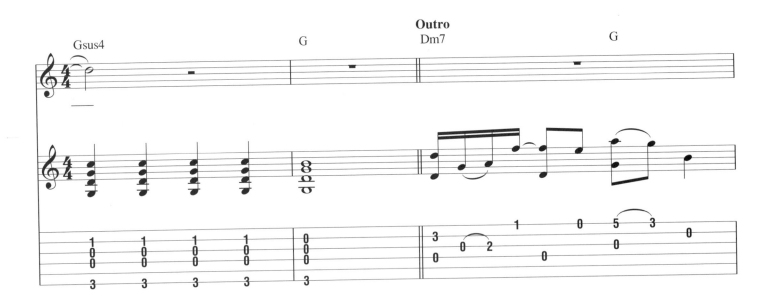

Take a look at me now. _____

rit.

rit.

Ain't No Sunshine

Words and Music by Bill Withers

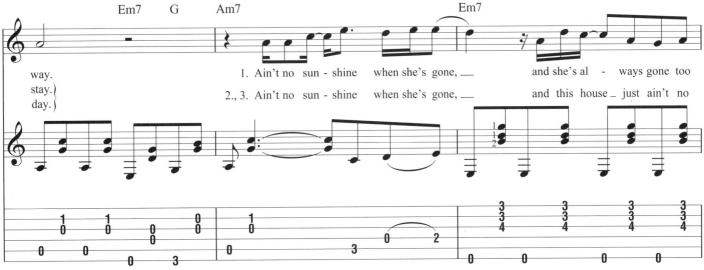

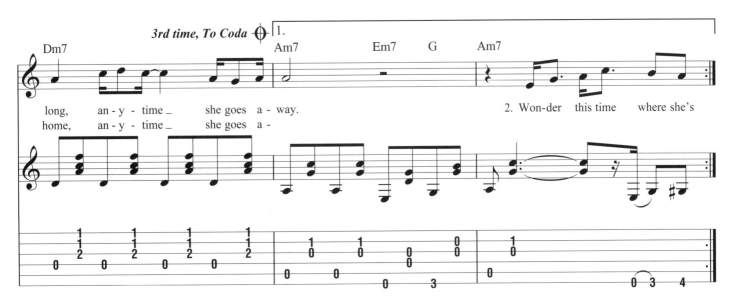

Copyright © 1971 INTERIOR MUSIC CORP.
Copyright Renewed
All Rights Controlled and Administered by SONGS OF UNIVERSAL, INC.
All Rights Reserved   Used by Permission

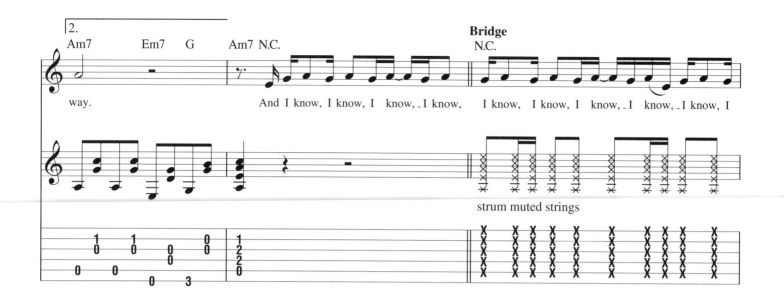

way. And I know, I know, I know, I know, I know, I know, I know, I know, I know, I

strum muted strings

know, I know, I know, I know, I know, I know, I know, I know, I know, I know, I know,

I know, I know, I know, I know, I know, I know, hey, I ought to leave the young thing a -

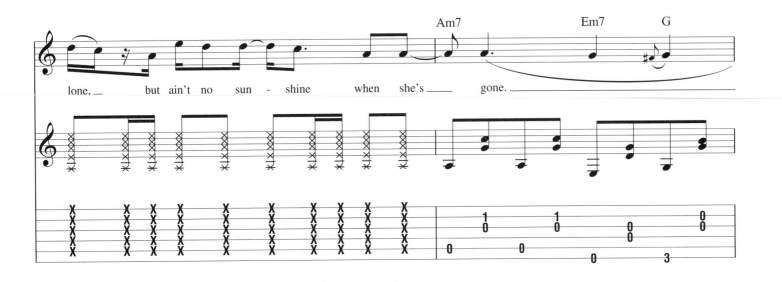

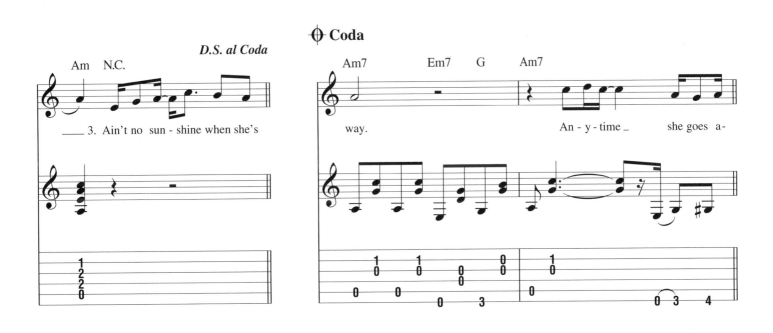

Angel

Words and Music by Sarah McLachlan

Drop D tuning:
(low to high) D-A-D-G-B-E

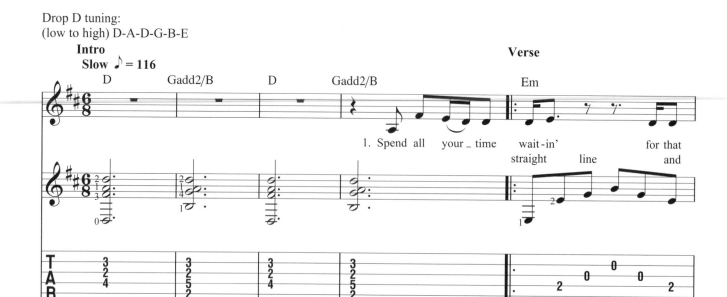

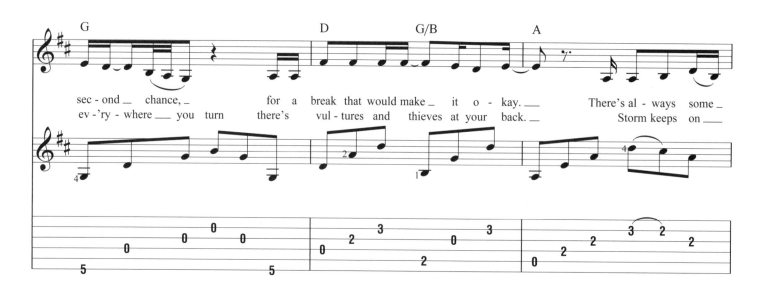

Copyright © 1997 Sony/ATV Music Publishing LLC and Tyde Music
All Rights Administered by Sony/ATV Music Publishing LLC, 8 Music Square West, Nashville, TN 37203
International Copyright Secured   All Rights Reserved

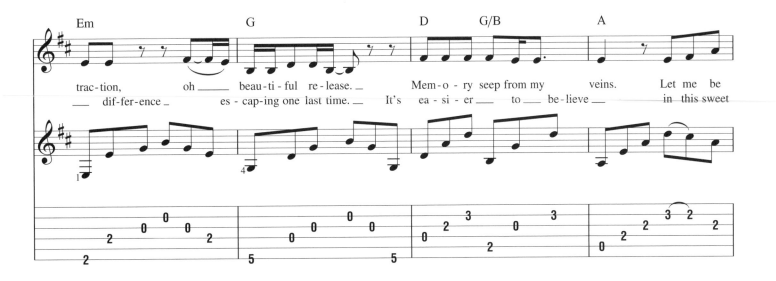

trac-tion, oh _____ beau-ti - ful re - lease. _____ Mem-o - ry seep from my veins. Let me be
_____ dif-fer-ence _____ es - cap-ing one last time. _____ It's ea - si - er _____ to _____ be-lieve _____ in this sweet

emp - ty, oh and weight-less and may - be I'll find some peace to-night _____ in the
mad-ness, oh this glo - ri - ous sad - ness that brings me to _____ my knees. In the

Chorus

arms of the an - gel. Fly a - way _____ from here, _____ from this

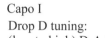
Black Hole Sun

Words and Music by Chris Cornell

Capo I
Drop D tuning:
(low to high) D-A-D-G-B-E

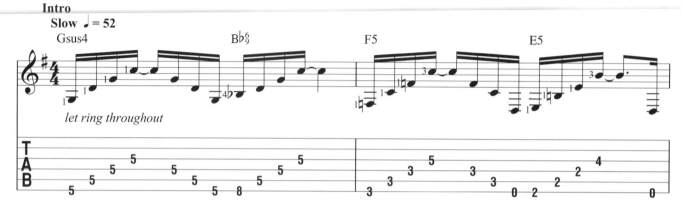

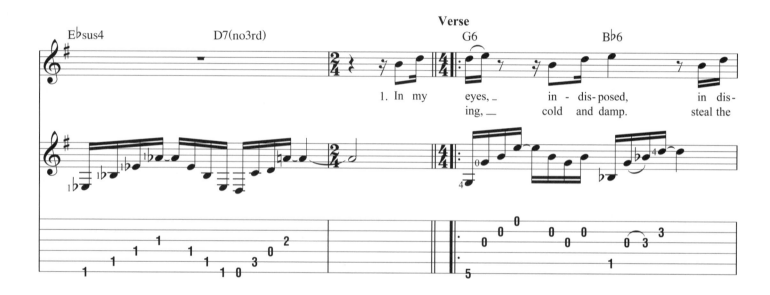

Copyright © 1994 You Make Me Sick I Make Music (ASCAP)
All Rights Administered by BMG Rights Management (US) LLC
All Rights Reserved   Used by Permission

Bless the Broken Road

Words and Music by Marcus Hummon, Bobby Boyd and Jeff Hanna

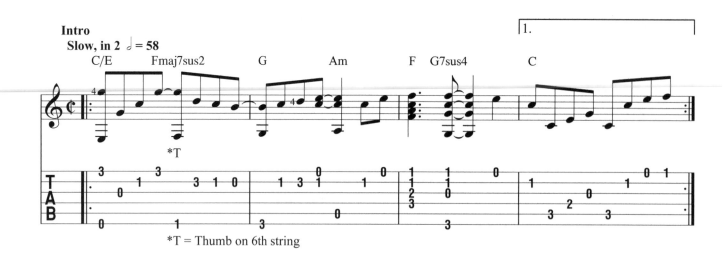

*T = Thumb on 6th string

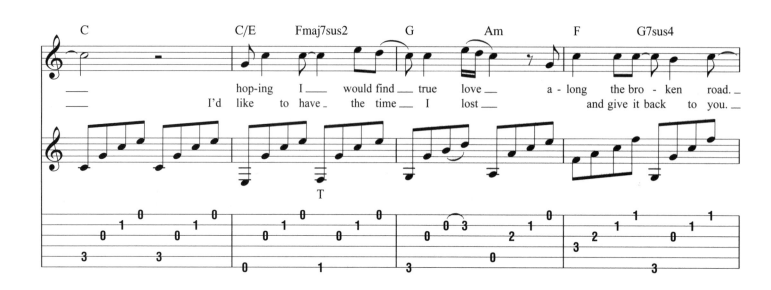

Copyright © 1994 by Universal Music - Careers, Floyd's Dream Music and Jeff Diggs Music
All Rights for Floyd's Dream Music Administered by Universal Music - Careers
All Rights for Jeff Diggs Music Administered by BUG Music, Inc., a BMG Chrysalis company
International Copyright Secured   All Rights Reserved

But I got lost __ a time __ or __ two, __ wiped my brow __ and kept
But you just smile __ and take __ my hand. __ You've been there, __ you

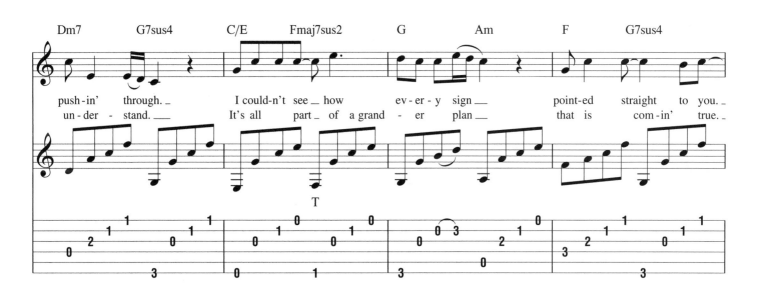

push-in' through. __ I could-n't see __ how ev-er-y sign __ point-ed straight to you. __
un-der - stand. __ It's all part __ of a grand - er plan __ that is com-in' true. __

Chorus

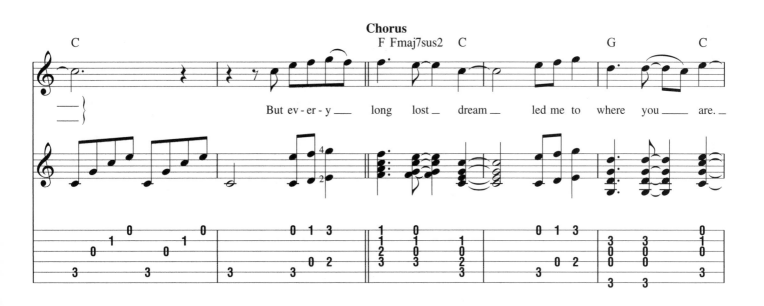

But ev-er-y __ long lost __ dream __ led me to where you __ are. __

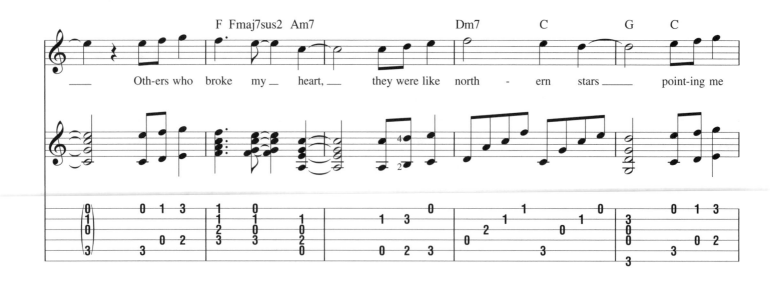

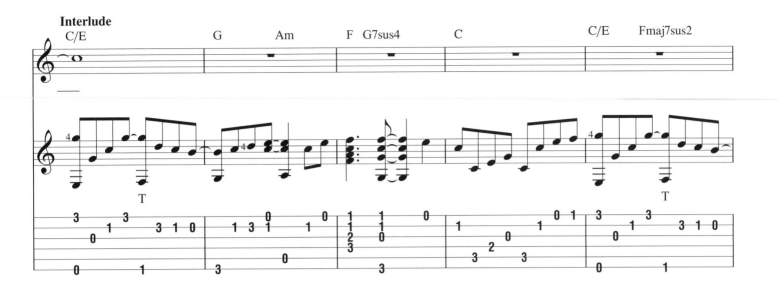

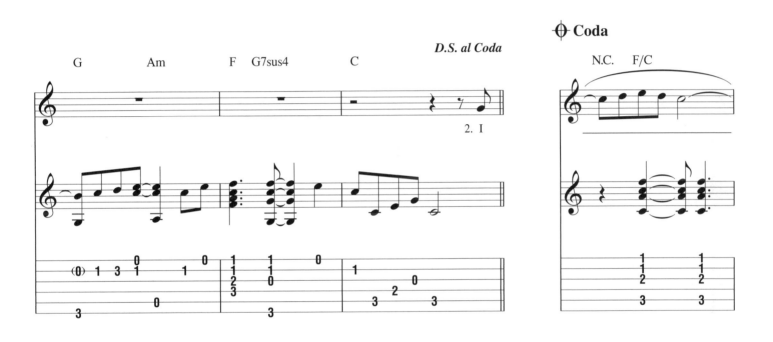

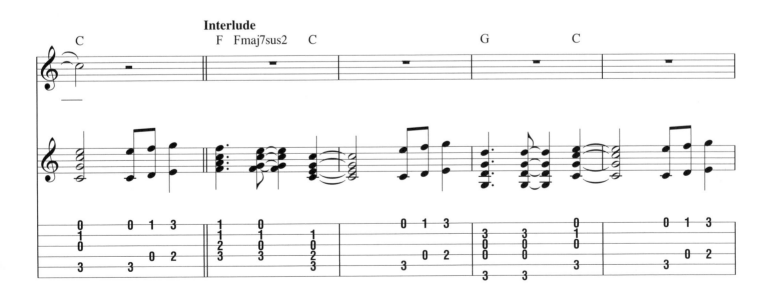

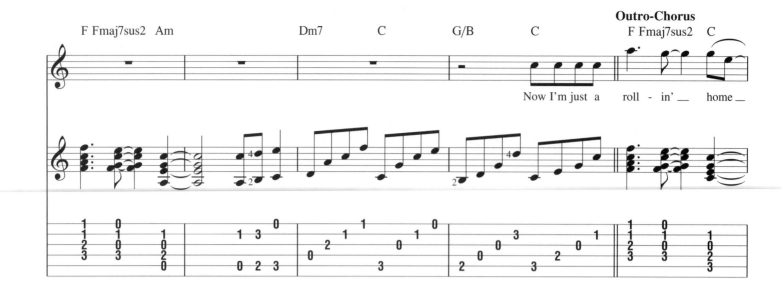

Outro-Chorus

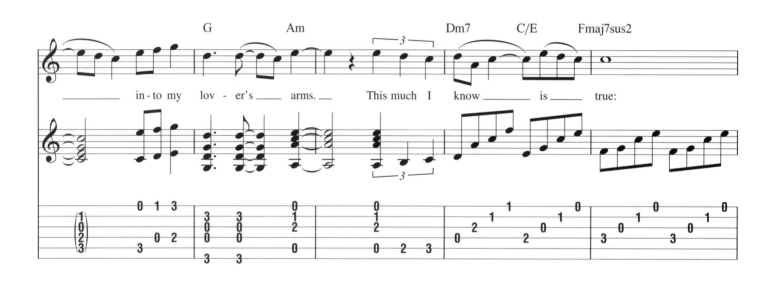

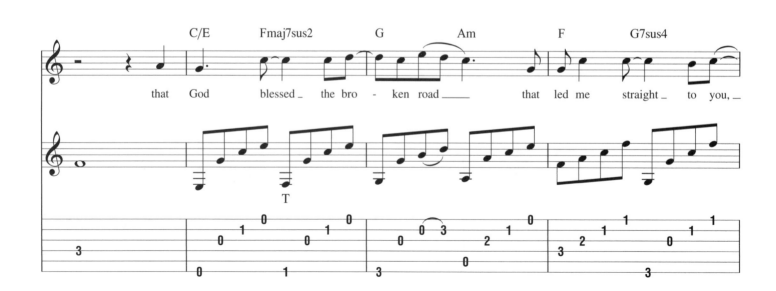

24

Bridge Over Troubled Water

Words and Music by Paul Simon

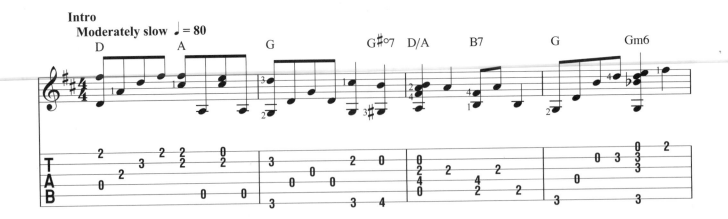

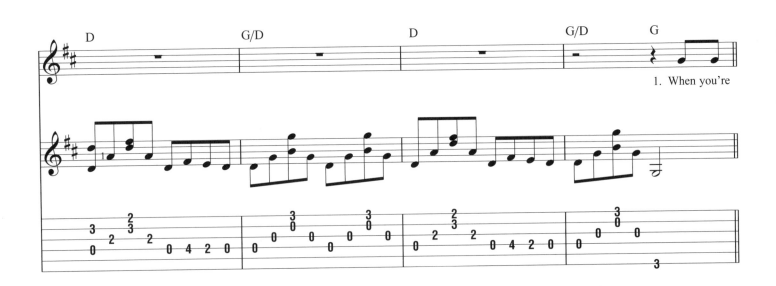

Copyright © 1969 Paul Simon (BMI)
Copyright Renewed
International Copyright Secured All Rights Reserved
Used by Permission

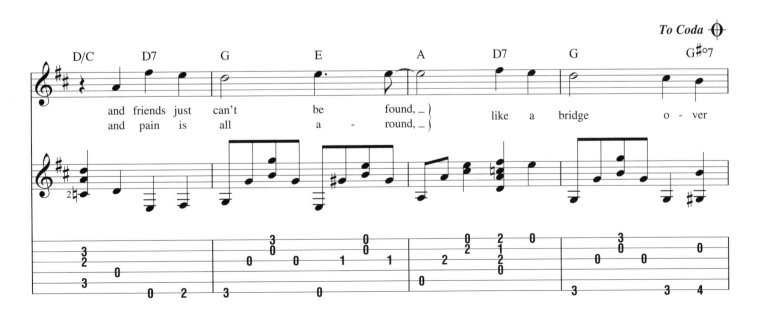

trou-bled wa - ter, I will lay me down. Like a bridge o - ver

trou-bled wa - ter, I will lay me down.

2. When you're

trou-bled   wa-ter,   I will lay   me   down. _____

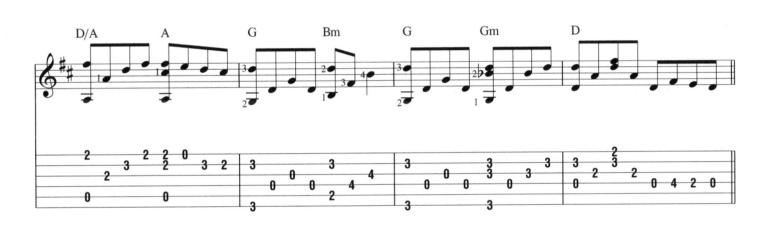

D.S. al Coda

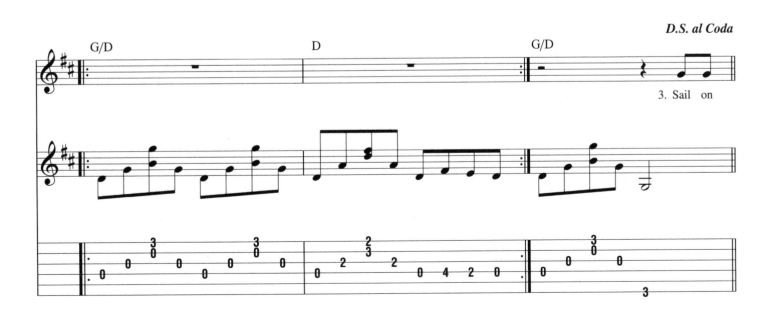

3. Sail on

Additional Lyrics

3. Sail on silver girl, sail on by.
   Your time has come to shine.
   All your dreams are on their way.
   See how they shine.
   Oh, if you need a friend,
   I'm sailing right behind.
   Like a bridge over troubled water,
   I will ease your mind.
   Like a bridge over troubled water,
   I will ease your mind.

Don't Know Why

Words and Music by Jesse Harris

Capo III

Intro

Moderately slow ♩ = 90

% Verse

1. I   wait-ed till ___ I   saw ___ the sun.   I don't know why ___   I did-
2. When I saw ___   the break ___ of day,   I wished that I ___ could fly ___
3., 4. *See additional lyrics*

n't come.
___ a-way

I left you by ___   the house ___ of fun. ___
'stead of kneel - ing   in   the   sand ___

I don't know why ___ I did-

Copyright © 2002 Sony/ATV Music Publishing LLC and Beanly Songs
All Rights Administered by Sony/ATV Music Publishing LLC, 8 Music Square West, Nashville, TN 37203
International Copyright Secured   All Rights Reserved

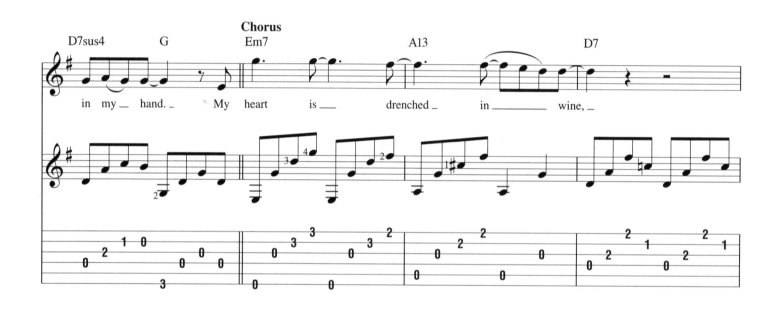

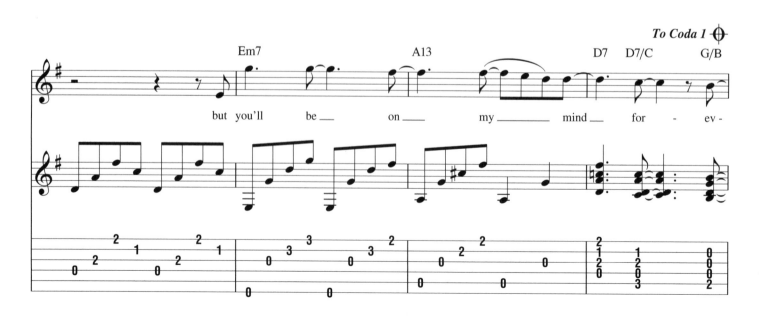

Coda 1

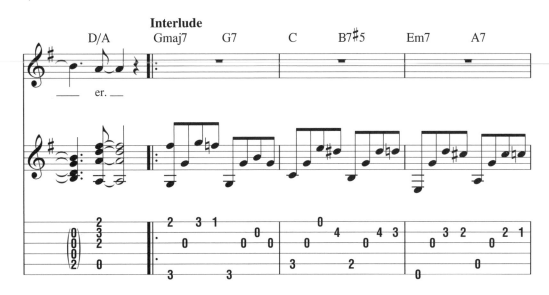

Coda 2

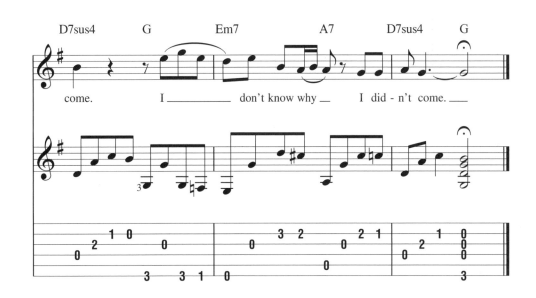

Additional Lyrics

3. Out across the endless sea,
   I would die in ecstacy.
   But I'll be a bag of bones
   Driving down the road alone.

4. Something has to make you run.
   I don't know why I didn't come
   I feel as empty as a drum.
   I don't know why I didn't come.
   I don't know why I didn't come.
   I don't know why I didn't come.

Every Breath You Take

Music and Lyrics by Sting

© 1983 G.M. SUMNER
Administered by EMI MUSIC PUBLISHING LIMITED
All Rights Reserved   International Copyright Secured   Used by Permission

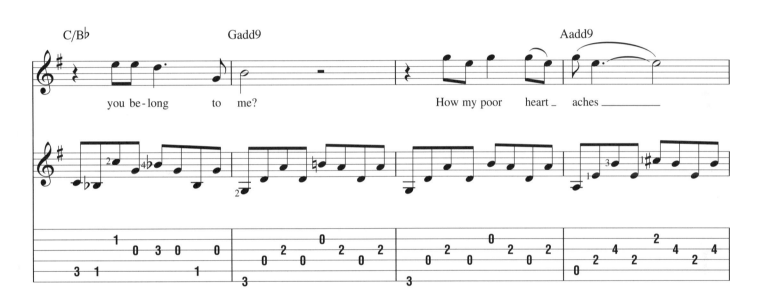

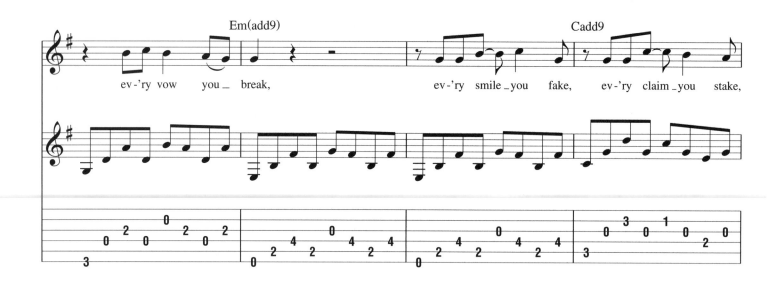

ev-'ry vow you _ break, ev-'ry smile _ you fake, ev-'ry claim _ you stake,

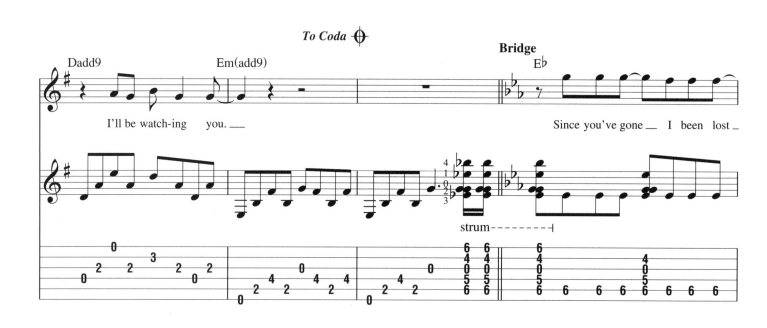

I'll be watch-ing you. _ Since you've gone _ I been lost _

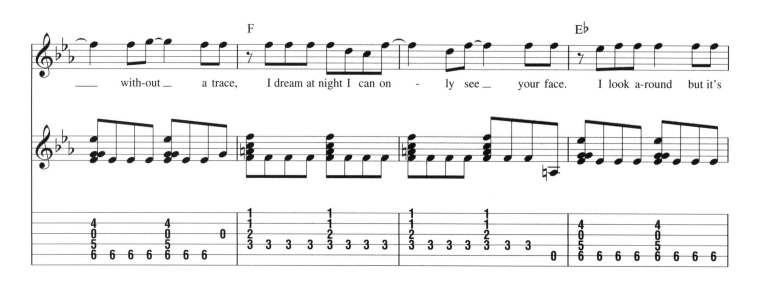

_ with-out _ a trace, I dream at night I can on - ly see _ your face. I look a-round but it's

you I can't _ re-place, I feel so cold and I long for your _ em-brace. I keep cry - ing ba-

- by, ba - by, please. ___

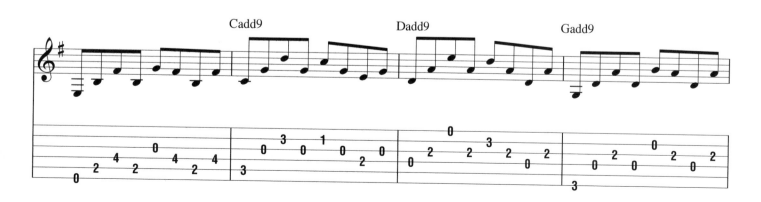

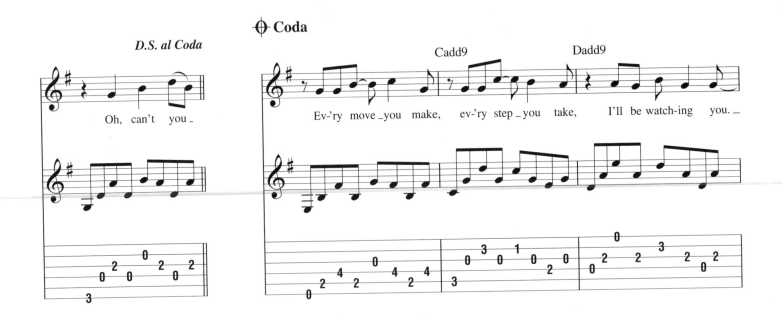

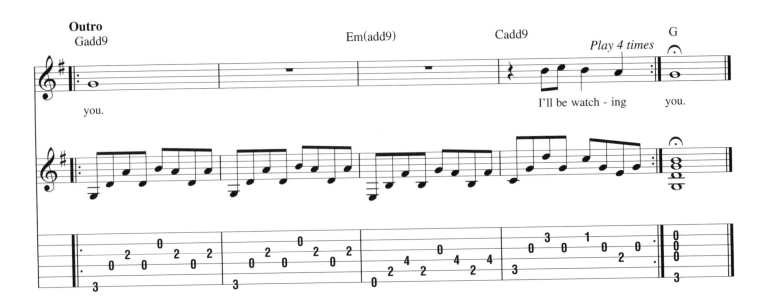

Fields of Gold
Music and Lyrics by Sting

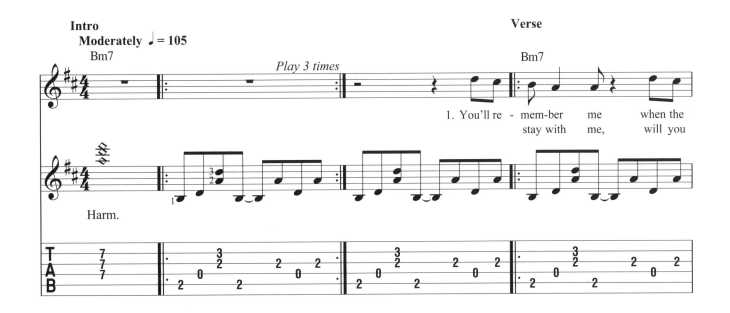

© 1993 STEERPIKE LTD.
Administered by EMI MUSIC PUBLISHING LIMITED
All Rights Reserved   International Copyright Secured   Used by Permission

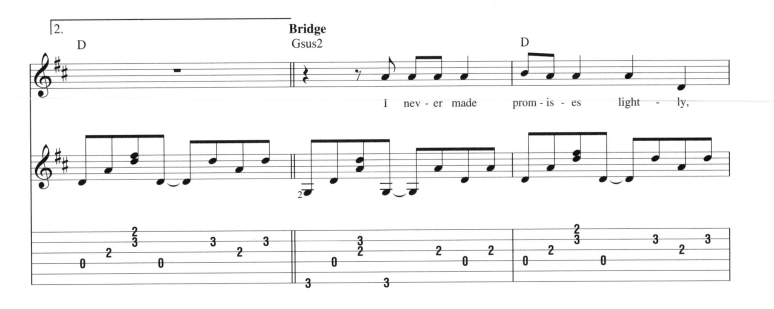

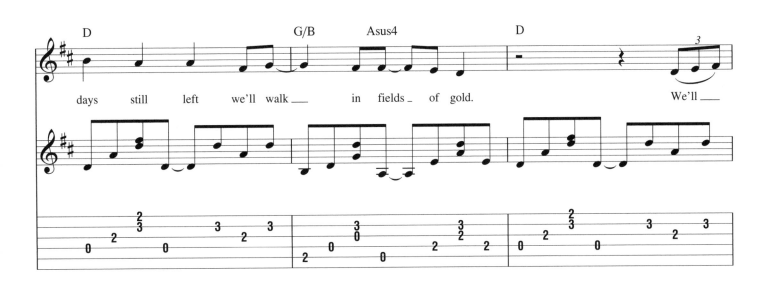

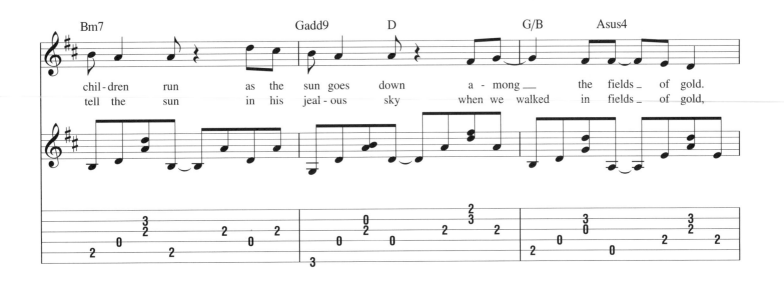

chil - dren run   as the sun goes down   a - mong __ the fields __ of gold.
tell the sun   in his jeal - ous sky   when we walked in fields __ of gold,

4. You'll re -

when __ we walked in fields __ of gold,

Outro

when we walked in fields __ of gold.

Play 3 times

The First Cut Is the Deepest

Words and Music by Cat Stevens

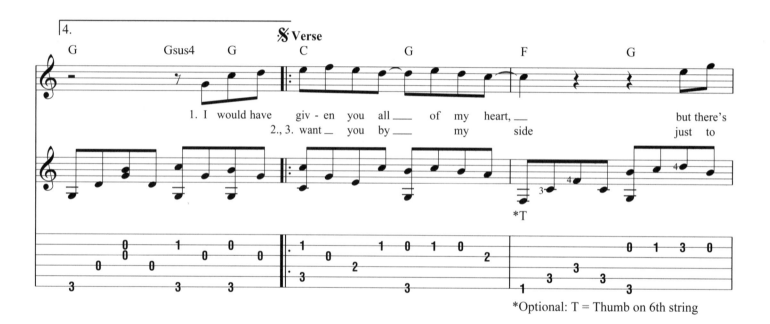

*Optional: T = Thumb on 6th string

Copyright ©1967 SALAFA LTD.
Copyright Renewed
All Rights in the U.S. and Canada Controlled and Administered by UNIVERSAL MUSIC CORP.
All Rights Reserved   Used by Permission

Free Bird

Words and Music by Allen Collins and Ronnie Van Zant

Intro
Slow ♩ = 55

Verse

1. If I leave __ here to-mor - row, __   would you still re-mem - ber
2. Bye - bye, __ ba - by, it's been   sweet now, ___ yeah, yeah.   Though this feel - in' I ___ can't

Copyright © 1973, 1975 SONGS OF UNIVERSAL, INC.
Copyrights Renewed
All Rights Reserved   Used by Permission

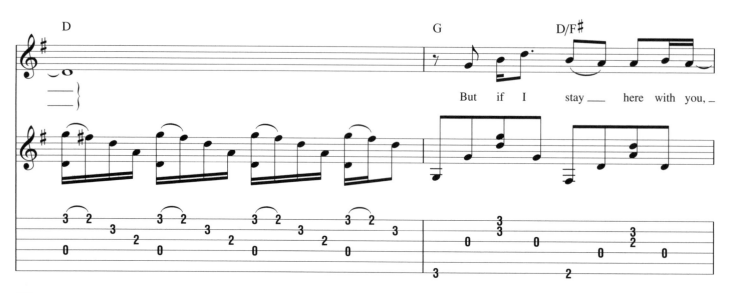

50

Outro

Hallelujah

Words and Music by Leonard Cohen

Capo V

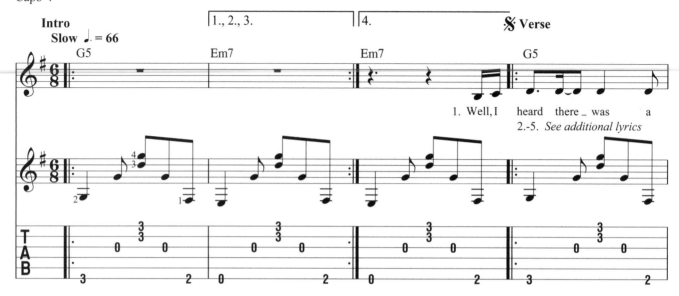

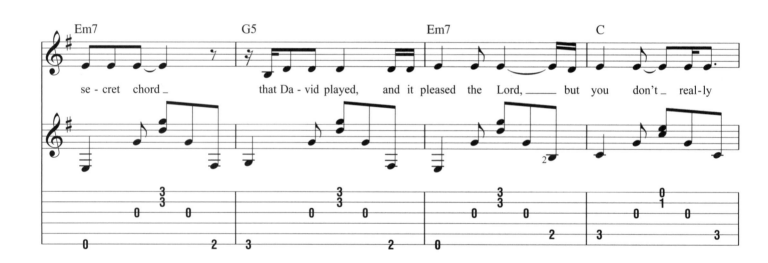

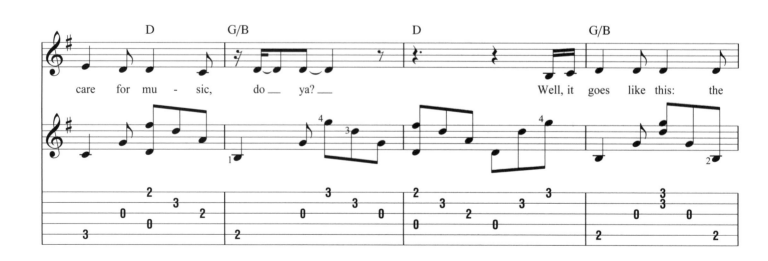

Copyright © 1995 Sony/ATV Music Publishing LLC
All Rights Administered by Sony/ATV Music Publishing LLC, 8 Music Square West, Nashville, TN 37203
International Copyright Secured   All Rights Reserved

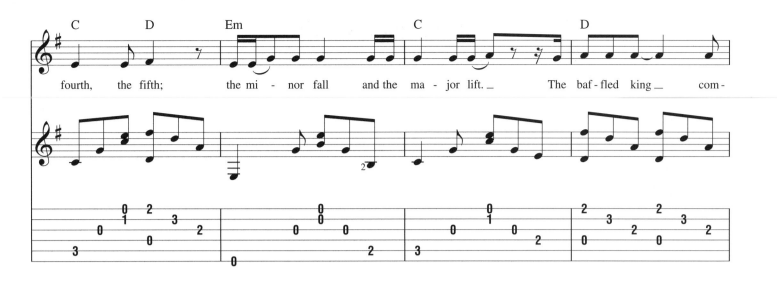

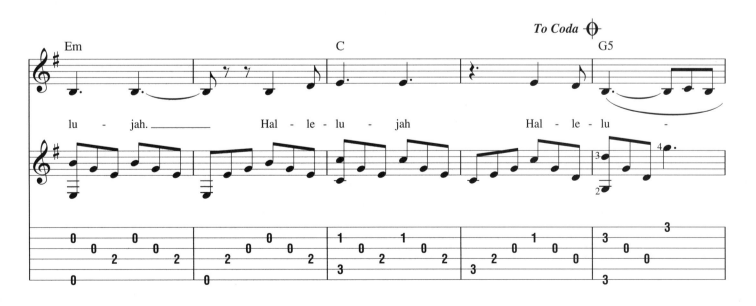

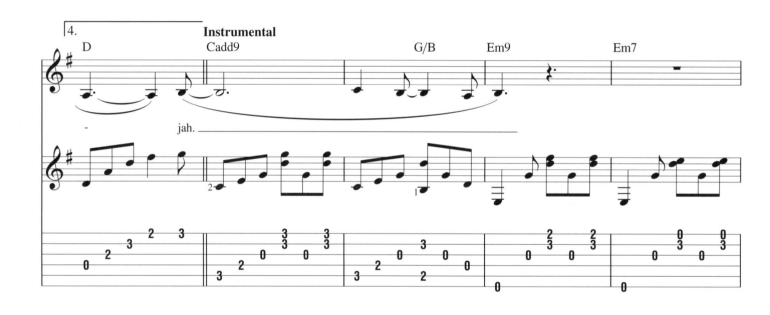

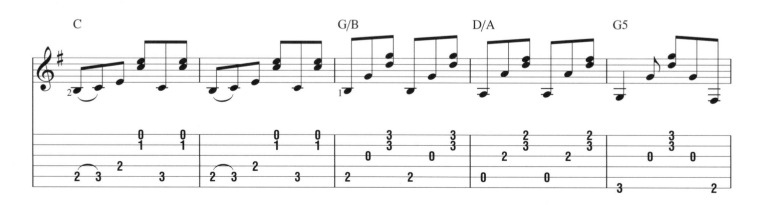

D.S. al Coda

Coda

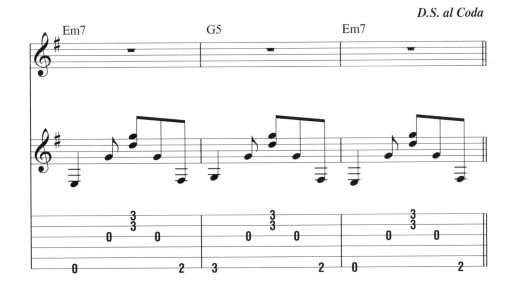

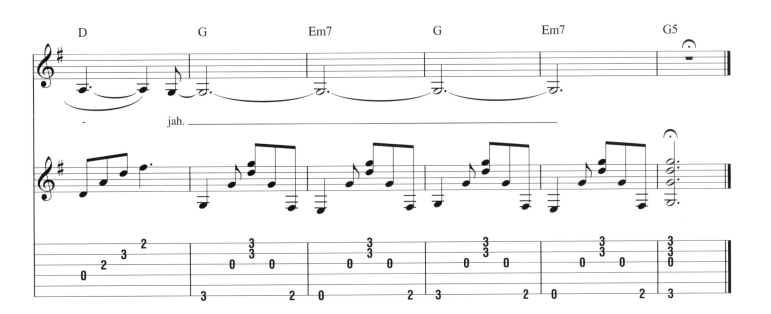

Additional Lyrics

2. Well, your faith was strong but you needed proof.
   You saw her bathing on the roof.
   Her beauty and the moonlight overthrew ya.
   As she tied you to her kitchen chair
   As she broke your throne and cut your hair
   And from your lips you drew the Hallelujah.

3. My baby, I've been here before.
   I've seen this room and I've walked this floor.
   You know, I used to live alone before I knew ya.
   And I've seen your flag on the marble arch,
   And love is not a victory march,
   It's a cold and it's a broken Hallelujah.

4. Well, there was a time when you let me know
   What's really going on below,
   But now you never show that to me, do ya?
   But remember when I moved in you,
   And the Holy Dove was moving too,
   And every breath we drew was Hallelujah?

5. Maybe there is a God above,
   But all I've ever learned from love
   Was how to shoot somebody who out-drew ya.
   And it's not a cry that you hear at night,
   And it's not somebody who's seen the light,
   It's a cold and it's a broken Hallelujah.

Have I Told You Lately

Words and Music by Van Morrison

Capo III

Intro

Slow ♩ = 72

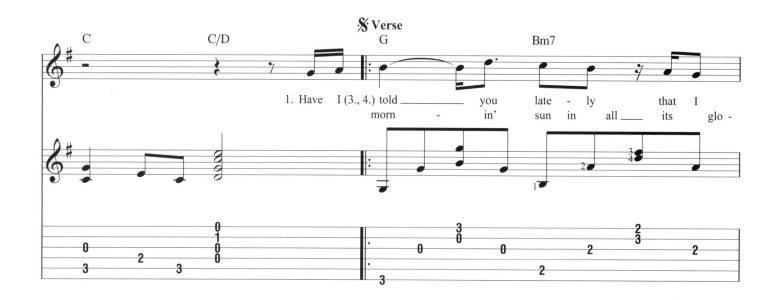

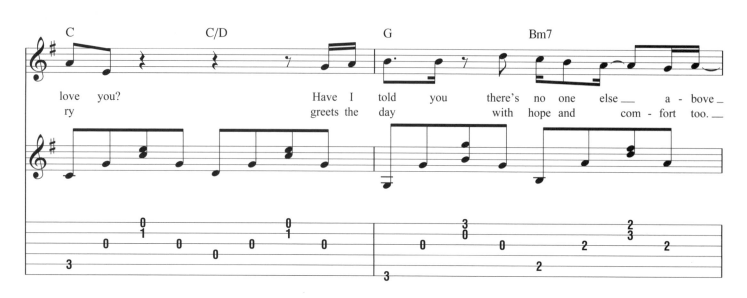

1. Have I (3., 4.) told ____ you late - ly that I

morn - in' sun in all ____ its glo -

love you?

ry

Have I told you there's no one else ____ a - bove ____

greets the day with hope and com - fort too. ____

Copyright © 1989 CALEDONIA PUBLISHING LTD.
All Rights for the U.S. and Canada Controlled and Administered by UNIVERSAL - SONGS OF POLYGRAM INTERNATIONAL, INC.
All Rights Reserved   Used by Permission

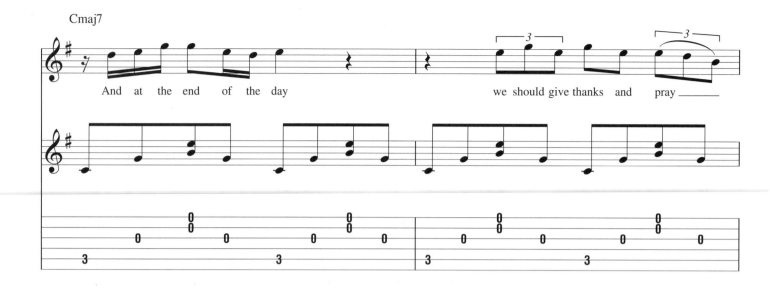

And at the end of the day we should give thanks and pray

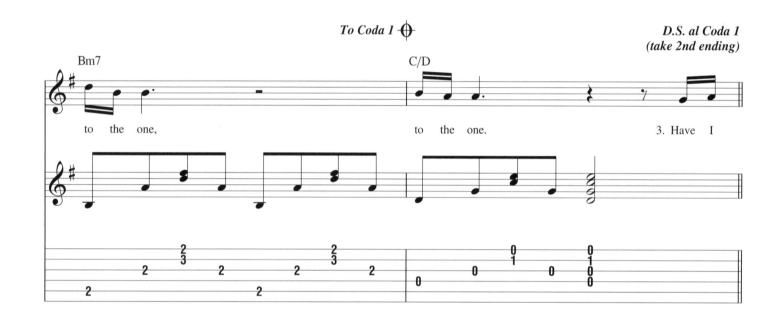

To Coda 1 ⊕   *D.S. al Coda 1*
(take 2nd ending)

to the one,   to the one.   3. Have I

⊕ **Coda 1**   ⊕ **Coda 2**

D.S. al Coda 2

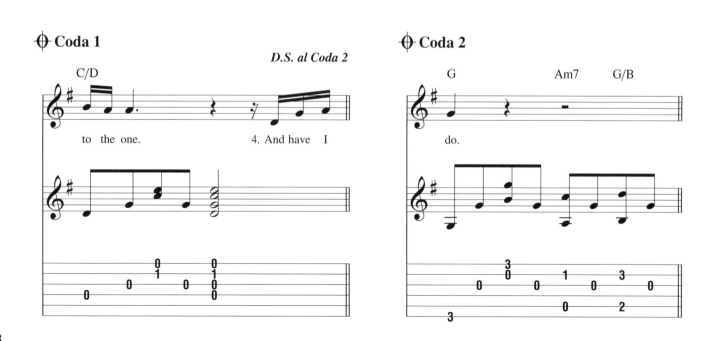

to the one.   4. And have I   do.

How Deep Is Your Love

from the Motion Picture SATURDAY NIGHT FEVER

Words and Music by Barry Gibb, Robin Gibb and Maurice Gibb

Capo III

Copyright © 1979 by Universal Music Publishing International MGB Ltd. and Crompton Songs LLC
All Rights for Universal Music Publishing International MGB Ltd. in the U.S. and Canada Administered by Universal Music - Careers
All Rights for Crompton Songs LLC Administered by Warner-Tamerlane Publishing Corp.
International Copyright Secured   All Rights Reserved

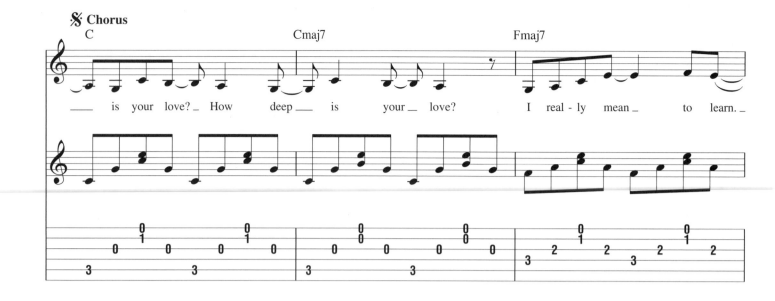

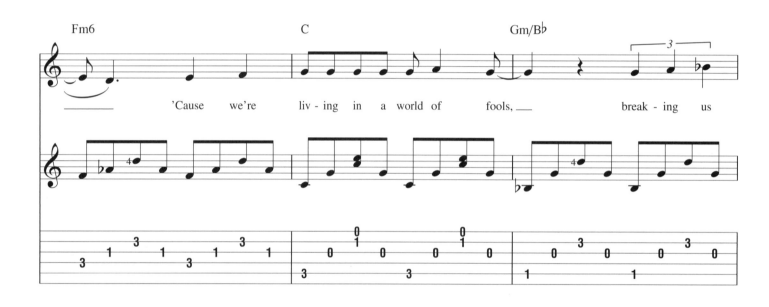

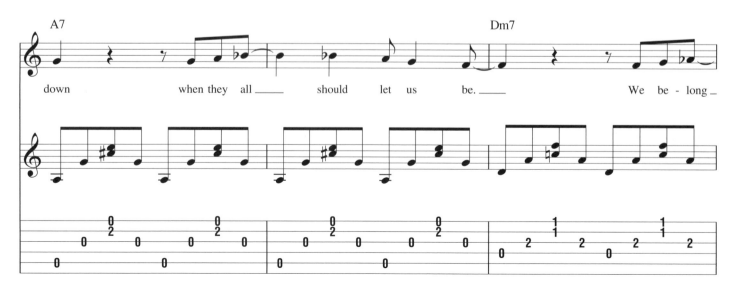

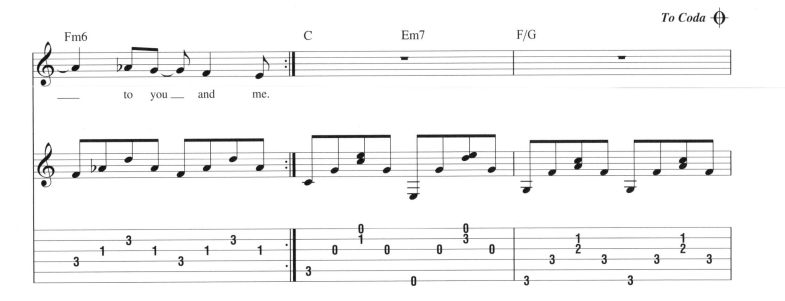

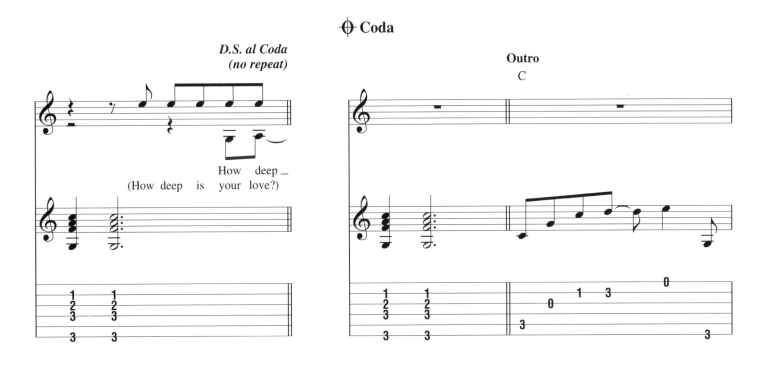

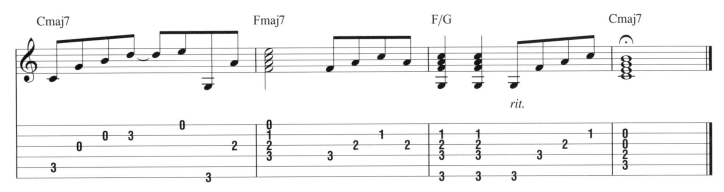

I Can't Make You Love Me

Words and Music by Mike Reid and Allen Shamblin

Capo III

Intro

Slow ♩ = 64

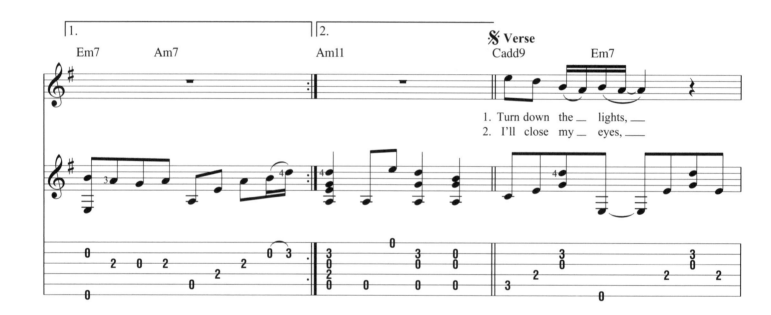

1. Turn down the __ lights, __
2. I'll close my __ eyes, __

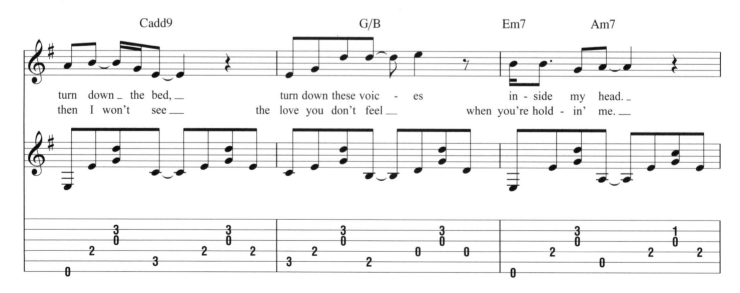

turn down __ the bed, __   turn down these voic - es   in - side my head. __
then I won't see __   the love you don't feel __   when you're hold - in' me. __

Copyright © 1991 ALMO MUSIC CORP., UNIVERSAL MUSIC - MGB SONGS and BRIO BLUES MUSIC
All Rights for BRIO BLUES MUSIC Administered by BMG RIGHTS MANAGEMENT (US) LLC
All Rights Reserved   Used by Permission

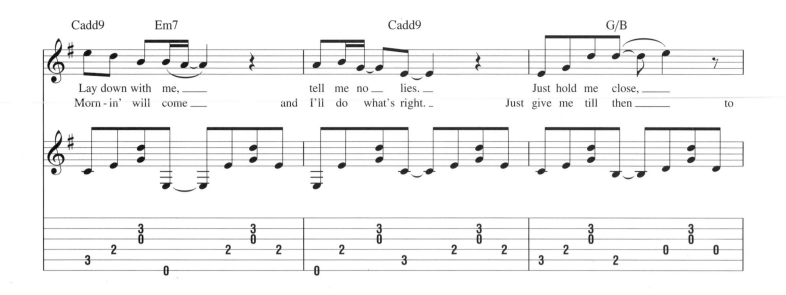

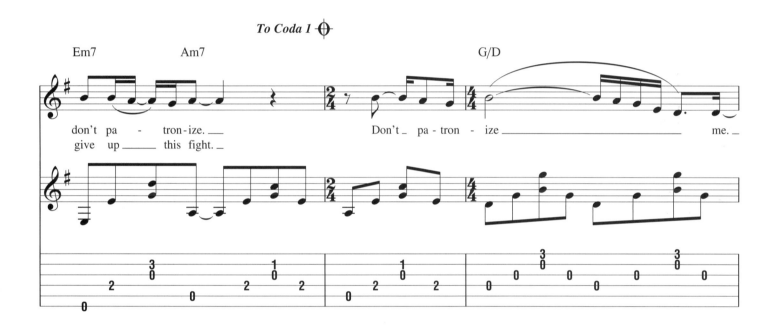

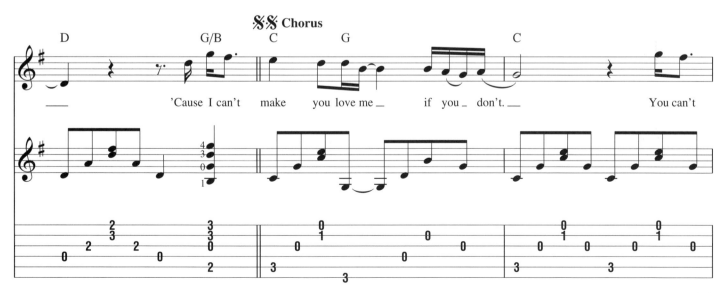

To Coda 2 ⊕

D.S. al Coda 1

Interlude

⊕ Coda 1

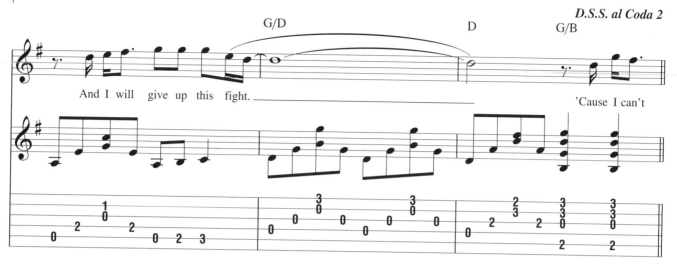

And I will give up this fight. _____

'Cause I can't

⊕ Coda 2
Outro

don't.

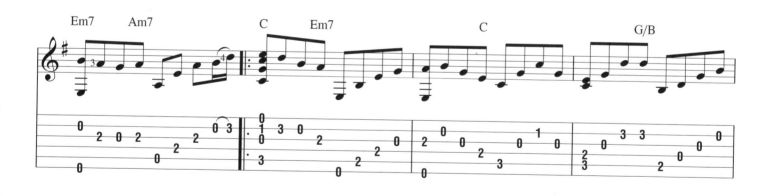

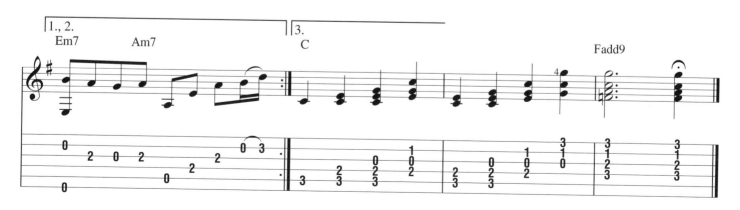

CD #2
TRACK 1

Imagine

Words and Music by John Lennon

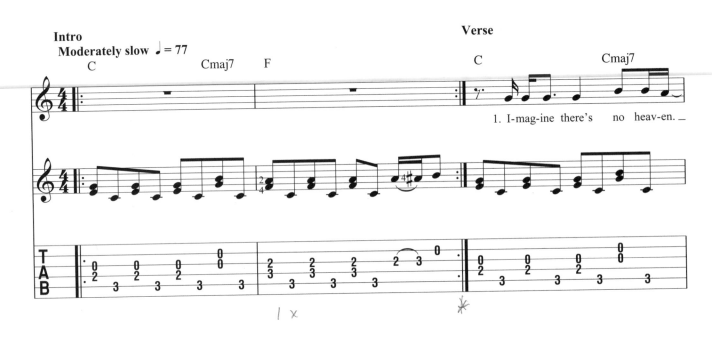

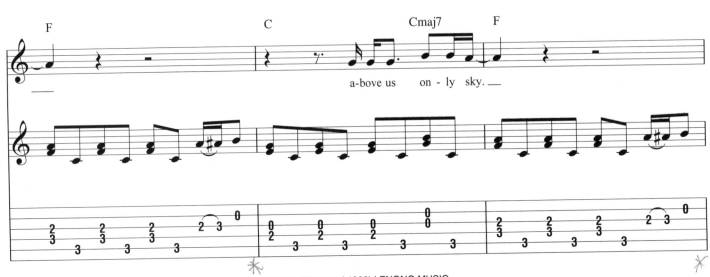

© 1971 (Renewed 1999) LENONO.MUSIC
All Rights in the U.S. and Canada Controlled and Administered by EMI BLACKWOOD MUSIC INC.
All Rights Reserved   International Copyright Secured   Used by Permission

Let It Be

Words and Music by John Lennon and Paul McCartney

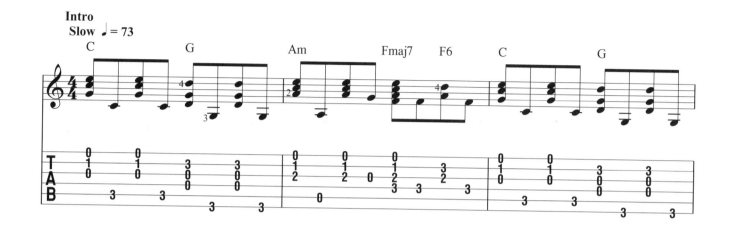

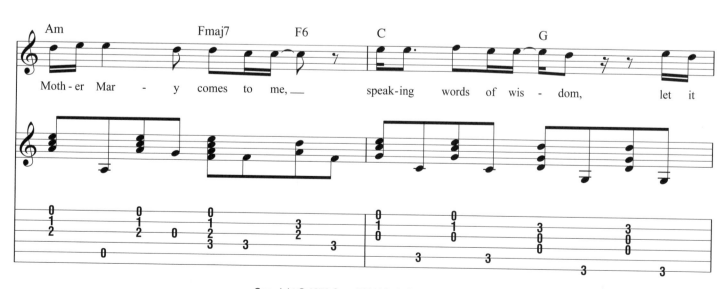

Copyright © 1970 Sony/ATV Music Publishing LLC
Copyright Renewed
All Rights Administered by Sony/ATV Music Publishing LLC, 8 Music Square West, Nashville, TN 37203
International Copyright Secured   All Rights Reserved

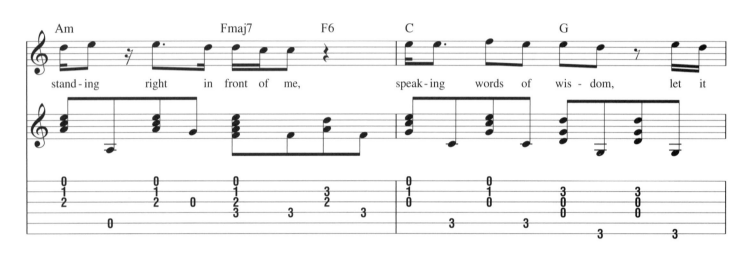

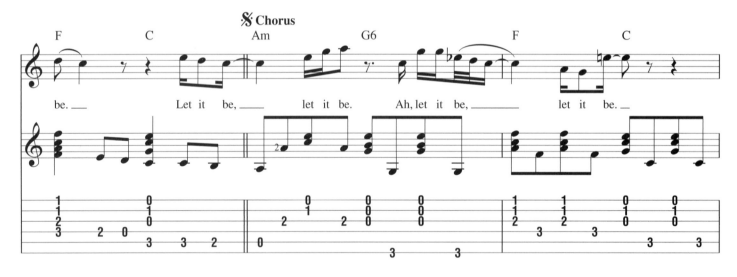

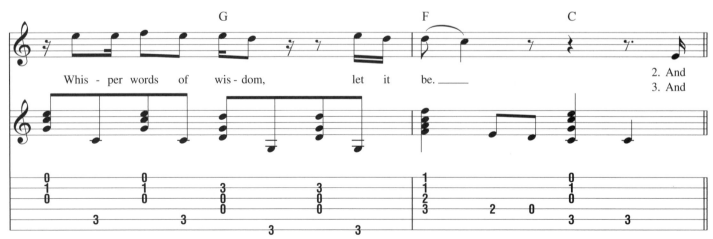

Verse

74

Nights in White Satin

Words and Music by Justin Hayward

1., 3. Nights in white sat - in, _____
2. Gaz - ing at peo - ple, _____

nev-er reach-ing the end.
some hand in hand.

Let - ters I've writ - ten _____
Just what I'm go - ing through

nev-er mean-ing to send. _____
they can't un - der-stand. _____

Beau - ty I'd al - ways missed
Some try to tell me _____

© Copyright 1967 (Renewed), 1968 (Renewed) and 1970 (Renewed) Tyler Music Ltd., London, England
TRO - Essex Music, Inc., New York, controls all publication rights for the U.S.A. and Canada
International Copyright Secured
All Rights Reserved Including Public Performance For Profit
Used by Permission

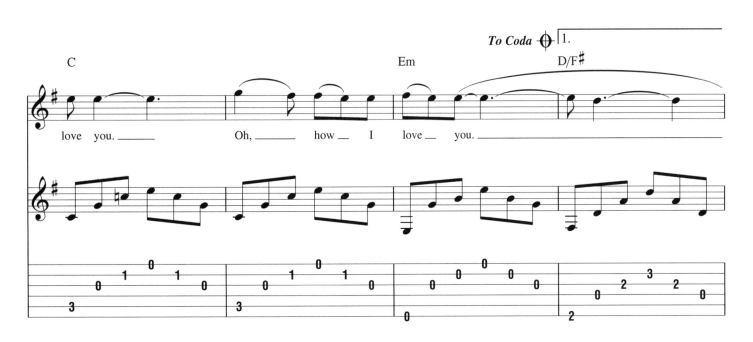

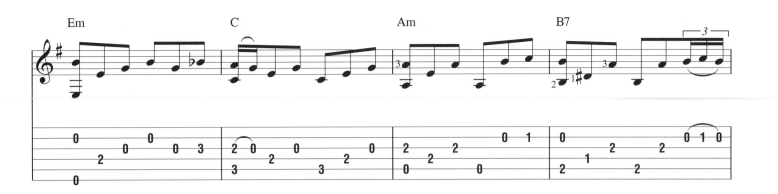

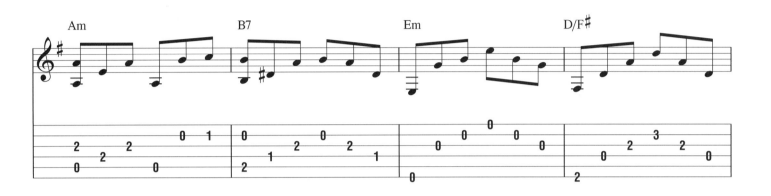

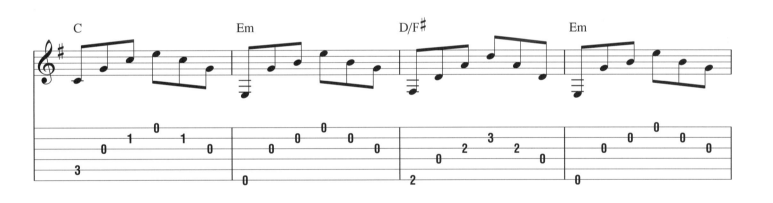

⊕ **Coda**

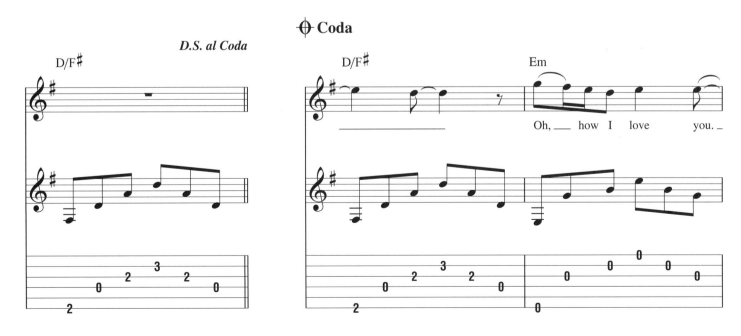

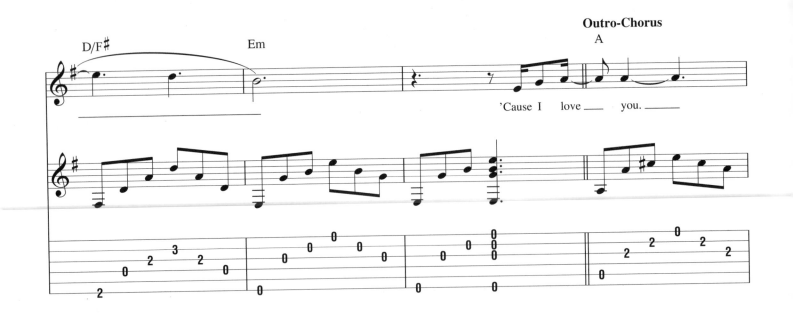

People Get Ready

Words and Music by Curtis Mayfield

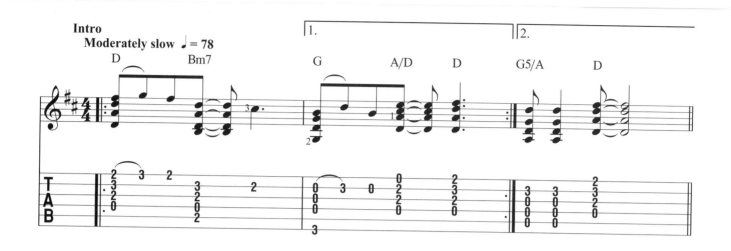

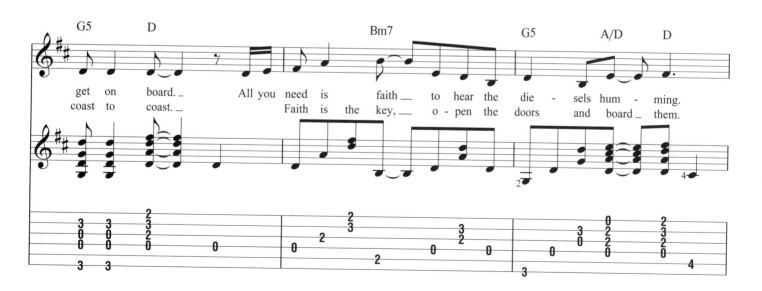

Copyright © 1964, 1965 Mijac Music and Warner-Tamerlane Publishing Corp.
Copyright Renewed
All Rights on behalf of Mijac Music Administered by Sony/ATV Music Publishing LLC, 8 Music Square West, Nashville, TN 37203
International Copyright Secured   All Rights Reserved

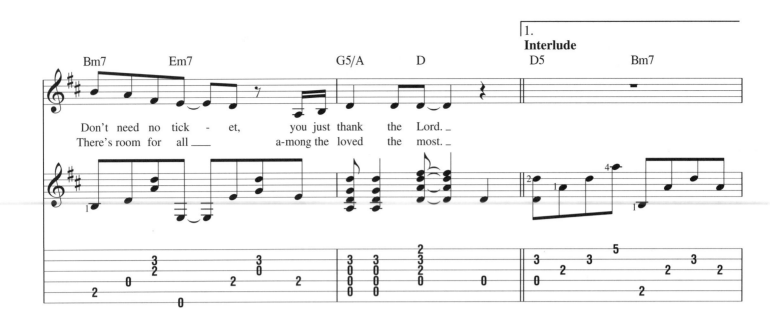

Don't need no tick - et, you just thank the Lord. _
There's room for all ___ a-mong the loved the most. _

2nd time, To Coda

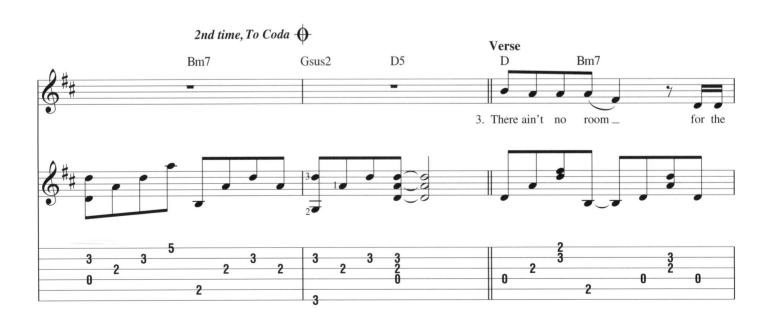

3. There ain't no room ___ for the

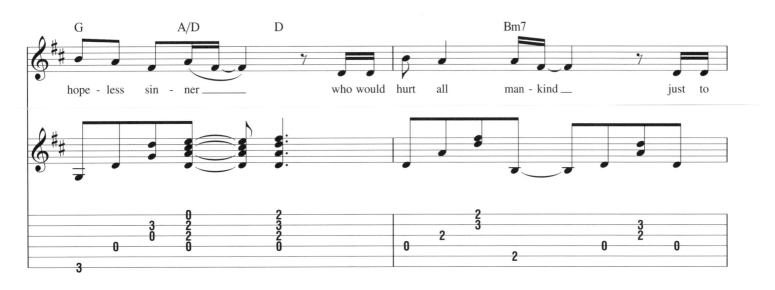

hope - less sin - ner _____ who would hurt all man - kind ___ just to

save _ his own. _ Have pit - y on those _ whose chanc - es grow thin - ner, 'cause there's

D.S. al Coda
(take 2nd ending)

 **Coda**

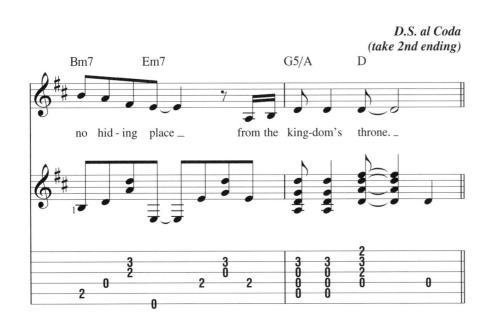

no hid - ing place _ from the king-dom's throne. _

Redemption Song

Words and Music by Bob Marley

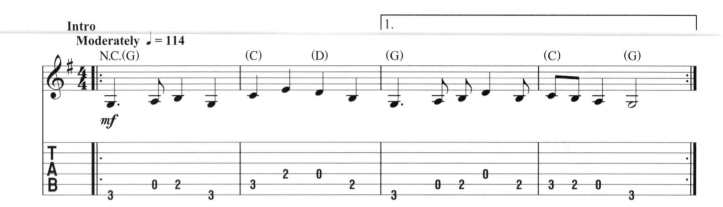

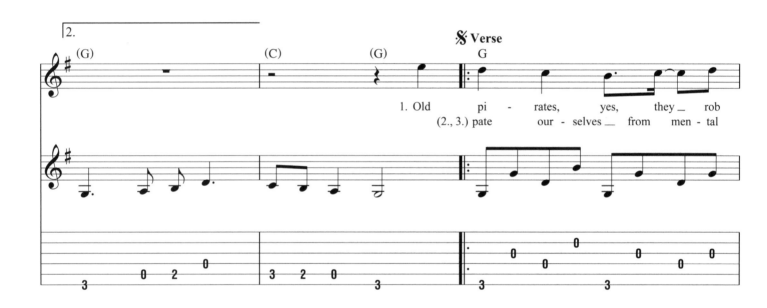

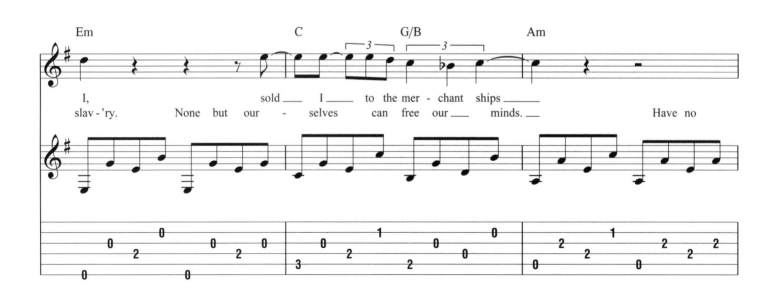

Copyright © 1980 Fifty-Six Hope Road Music Ltd. and Odnil Music Ltd.
All Rights in North America Administered by Blue Mountain Music Ltd./Irish Town Songs (ASCAP)
and throughout the rest of the world by Blue Mountain Music Ltd. (PRS)
All Rights Reserved

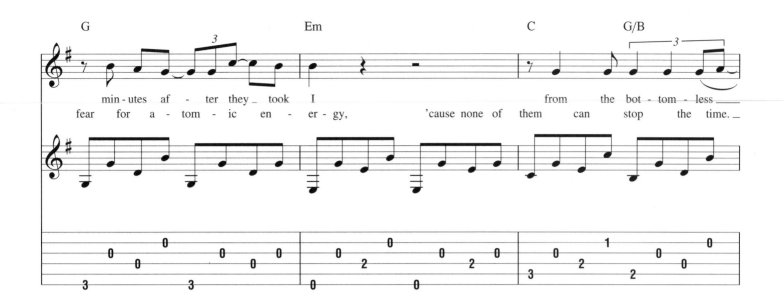

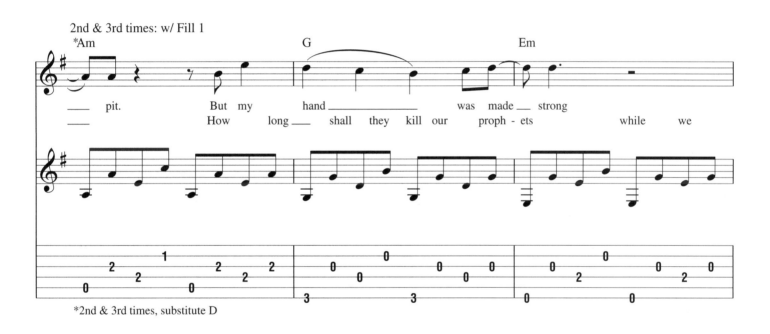

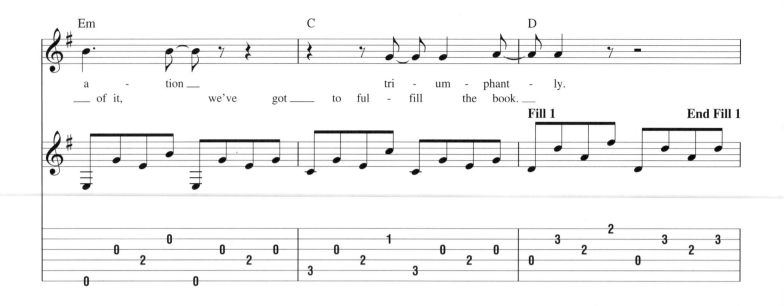

a - tion ___ tri - um - phant - ly.
___ of it, we've got ___ to ful - fill the book. ___

Fill 1   End Fill 1

To Coda ⊕

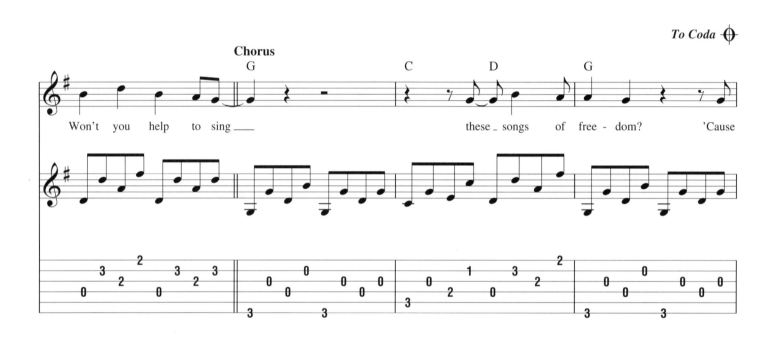

Chorus

Won't you help to sing ___ these ___ songs of free - dom? 'Cause

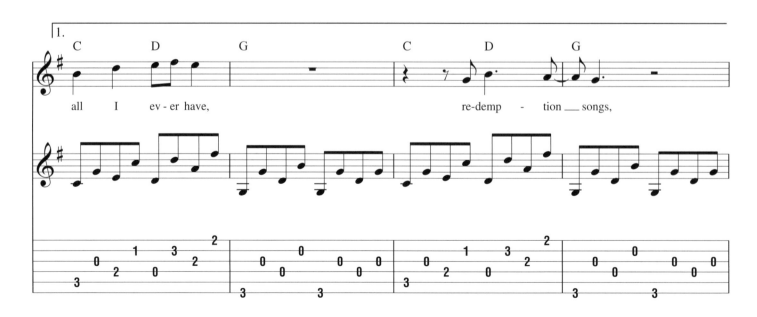

1.

all I ev - er have, re-demp - tion ___ songs,

re - demp - tion ___ songs.
2. E - man - ci -

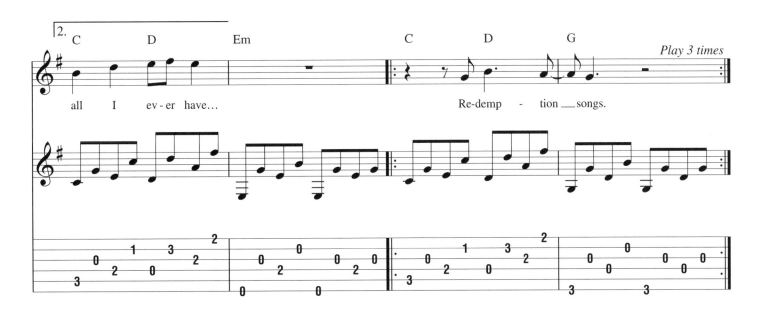

all I ev - er have…
Re-demp - tion ___ songs.

Interlude

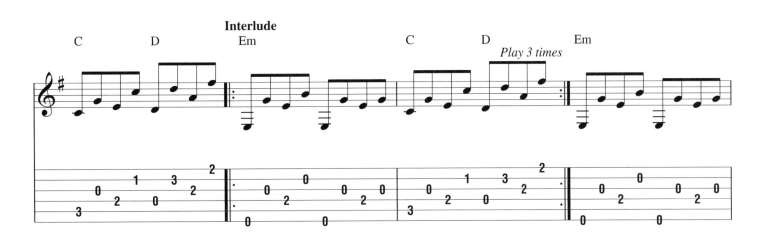

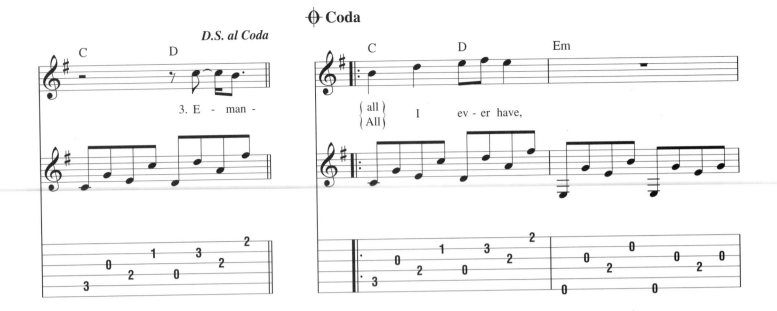

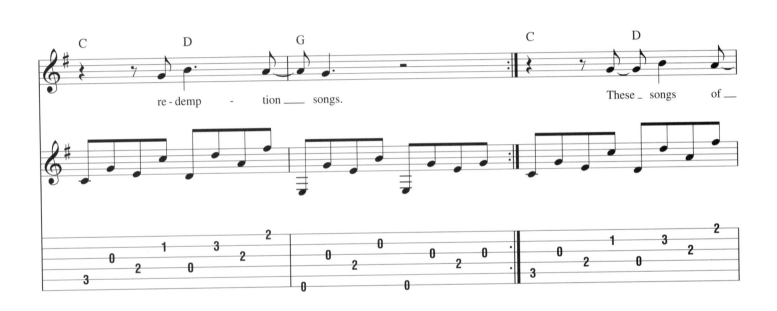

Right Here Waiting

Words and Music by Richard Marx

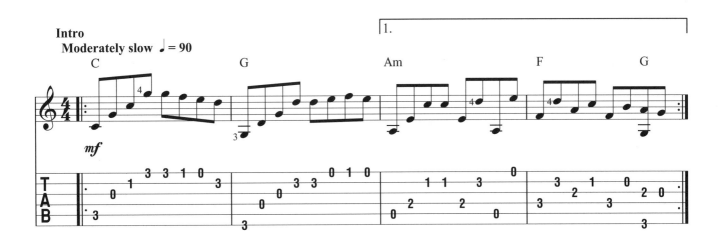

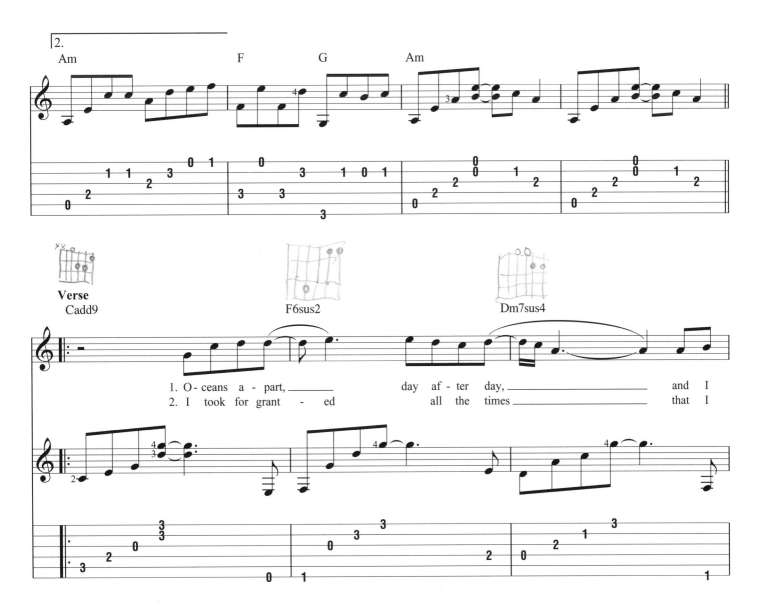

Copyright © 1989 Chrysalis Music
All Rights Administered by Chrysalis Music Group Inc., a BMG Chrysalis company
All Rights Reserved   Used by Permission

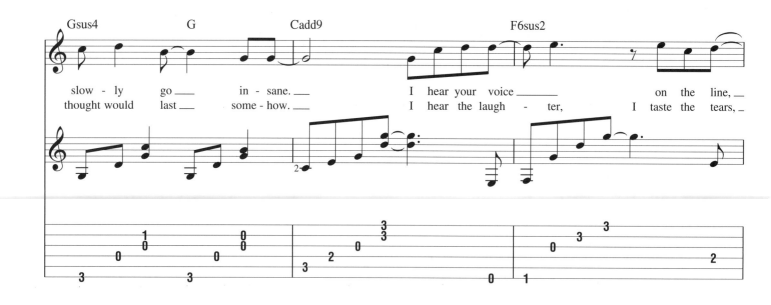

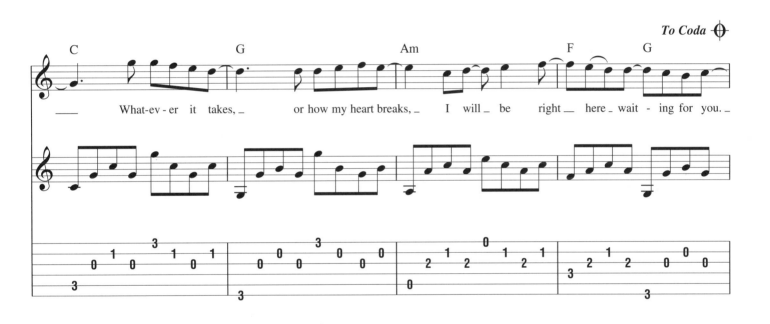

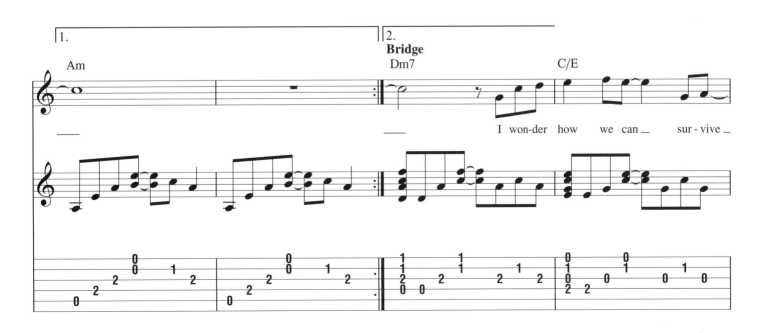

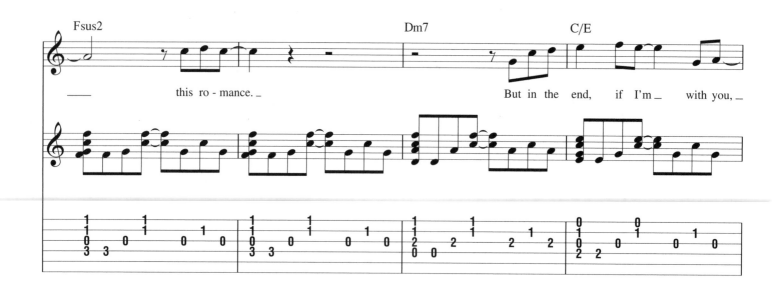

this ro - mance. _

But in the end, if I'm _ with you, _

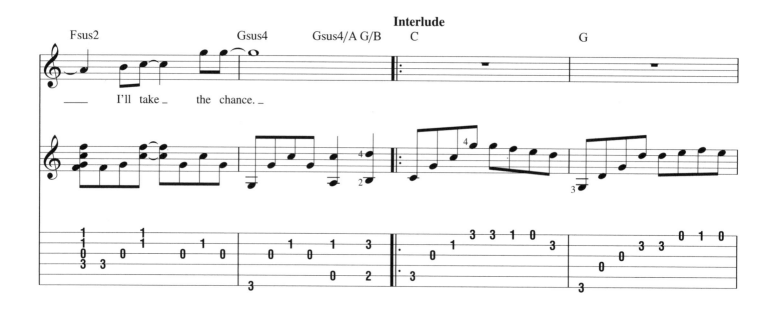

I'll take _ the chance. _

Interlude

Pre-Chorus

Oh, can't you see ___ it, ba - by? ___ You've got me go - in' cra - zy. ___

Coda

Outro

Wait-ing for you. _

The Scientist

Words and Music by Guy Berryman, Jon Buckland,
Will Champion and Chris Martin

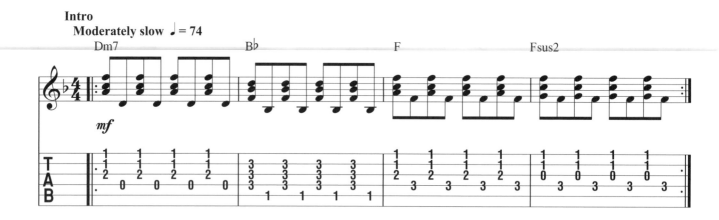

1. Come up to meet ___ you, tell you I'm sor - ry, you don't know how love -
2. I was just guess - ing at num-bers and fig - ures, pull - ing the puz -

- ly you are. _____ I had to find ___ you, tell you I need ___
- zles a - part. _____ Ques-tions of sci - ence, sci - ence and pro -

Copyright © 2002 by Universal Music Publishing MGB Ltd.
All Rights in the United States Administered by Universal Music - MGB Songs
International Copyright Secured   All Rights Reserved

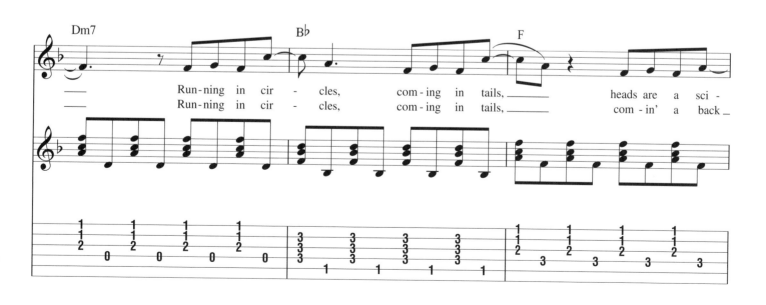

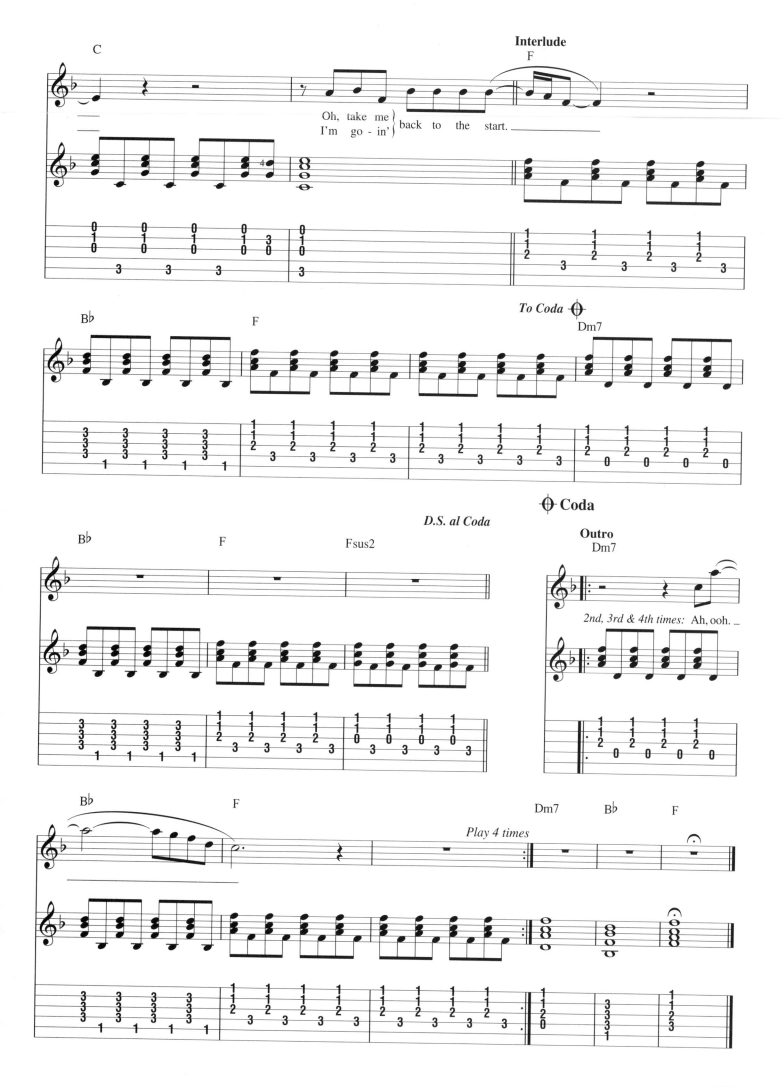

Someone Like You

Words and Music by Adele Adkins and Dan Wilson

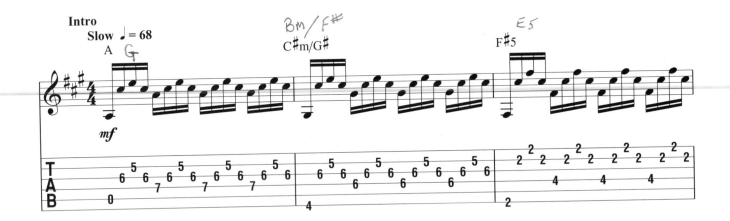

Copyright © 2011 UNIVERSAL MUSIC PUBLISHING LTD., CHRYSALIS MUSIC and SUGAR LAKE MUSIC
All Rights for UNIVERSAL MUSIC PUBLISHING LTD. in the U.S. and Canada Controlled and Administered by
UNIVERSAL - SONGS OF POLYGRAM INTERNATIONAL, INC.
All Rights for CHRYSALIS MUSIC and SUGAR LAKE MUSIC Administered by
CHRYSALIS MUSIC GROUP INC., A BMG CHRYSALIS COMPANY
All Rights Reserved   Used by Permission

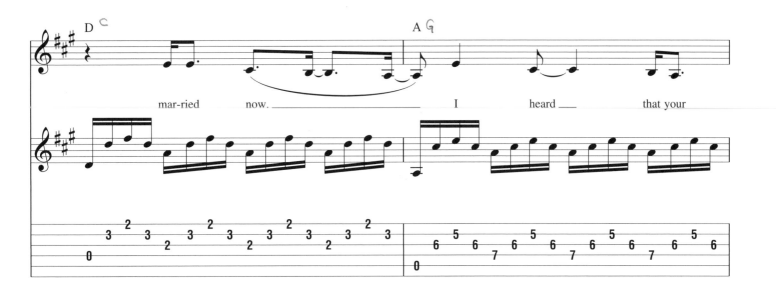

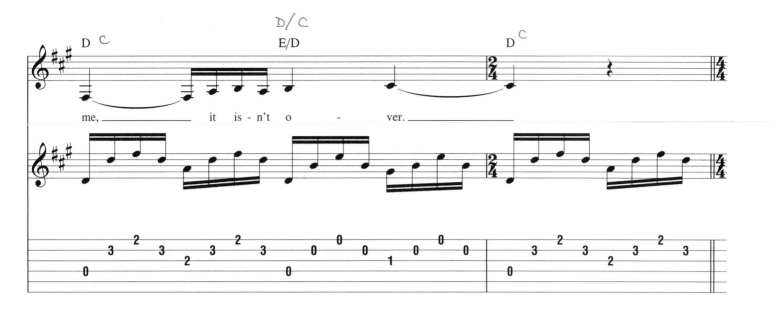

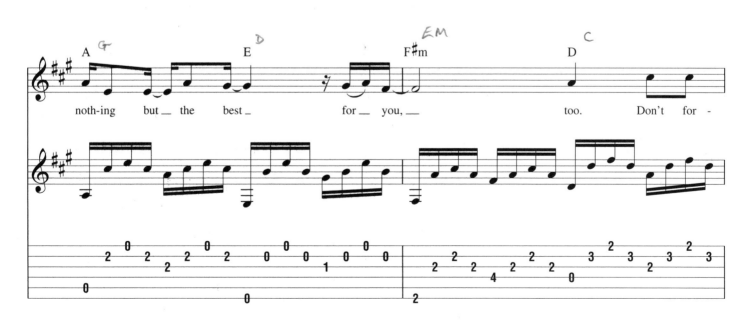

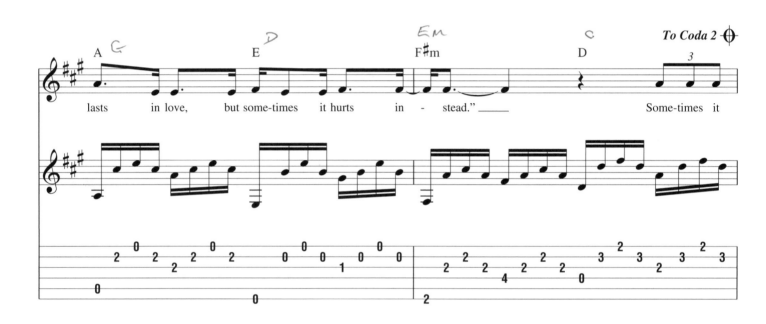

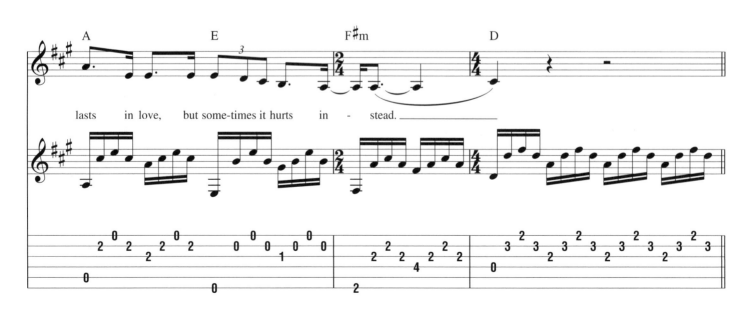

Verse

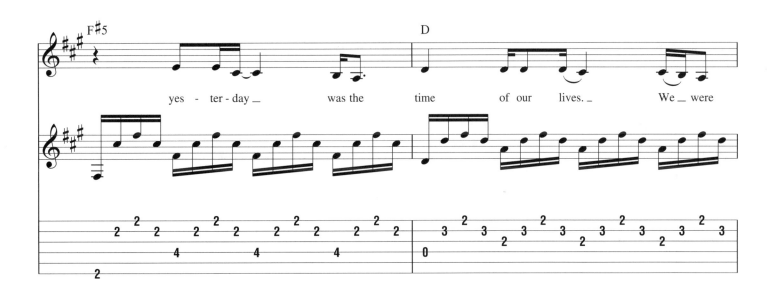

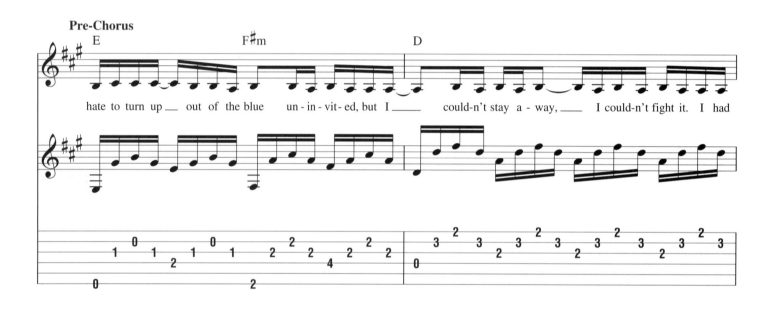

Pre-Chorus

D.S. al Coda 1

Coda 1

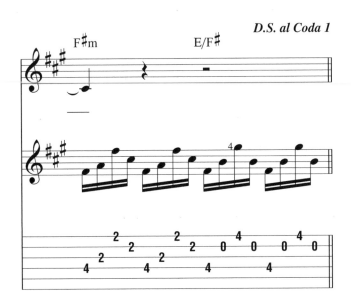

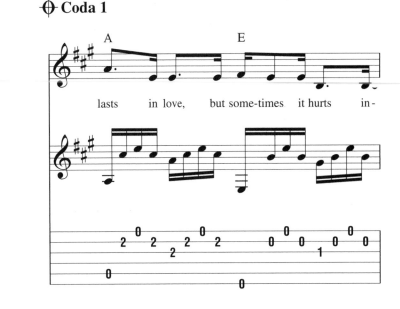

lasts   in love,   but some-times   it hurts   in -

Bridge

- stead." _____   Noth-ing   com-pares,   no   wor-ries   or cares,   re -

grets and mis-takes, they're mem-or-ies made.   Who would have known   how ____   bit-ter

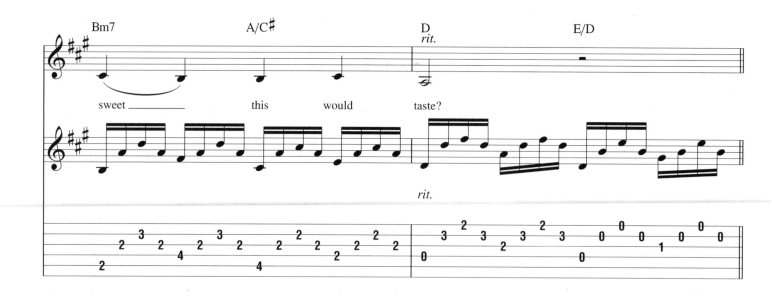

lasts in love, but some-times it hurts in - stead." _____

Coda 2

lasts in love, but some-times it hurts in - stead. _____

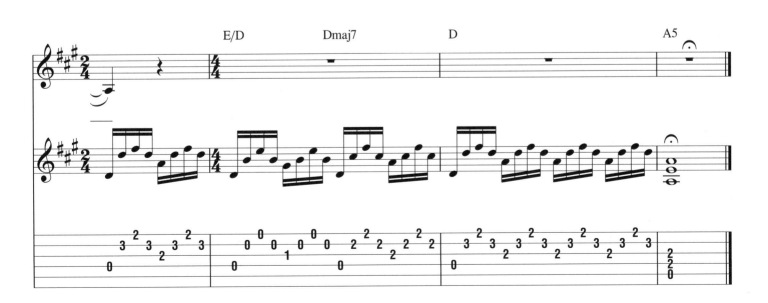

CD #2
TRACK 9

Walking in Memphis
Words and Music by Marc Cohn

Copyright © 1991 Sony/ATV Music Publishing LLC
All Rights Administered by Sony/ATV Music Publishing LLC, 8 Music Square West, Nashville, TN 37203
International Copyright Secured   All Rights Reserved

*W. _____ C. Handy,

*Dou - ble - u

*2nd & 3rd times

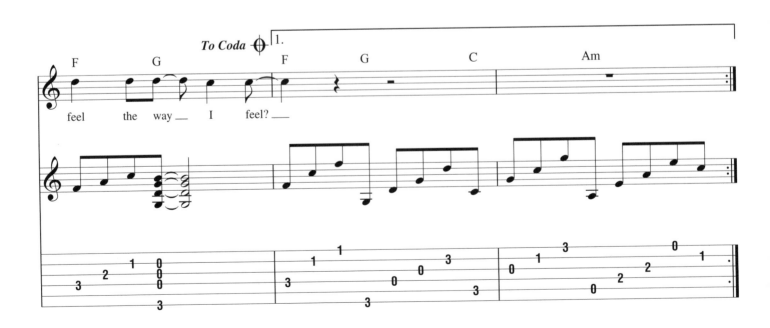

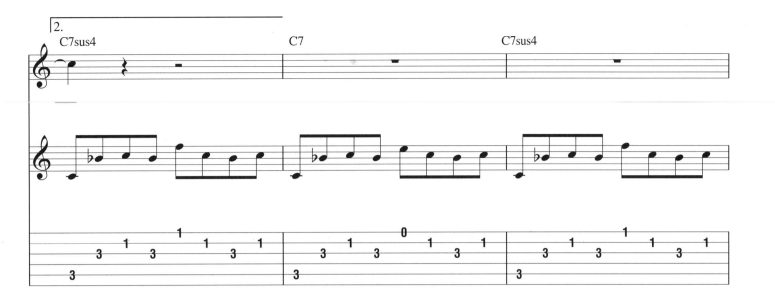

Bridge

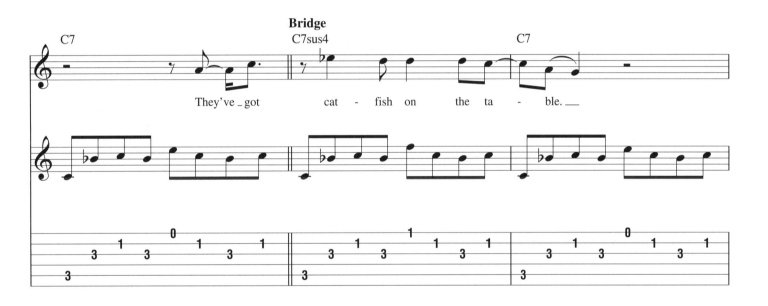

They've _ got cat - fish on the ta - ble. _

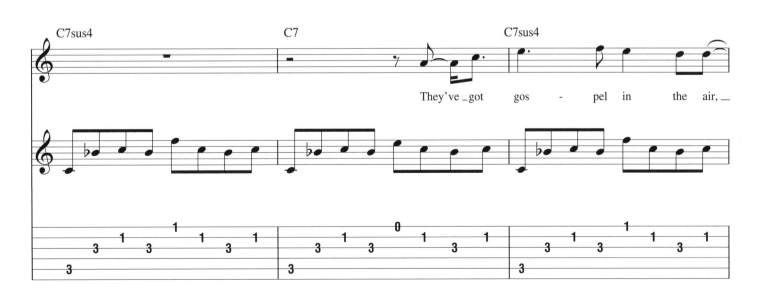

They've _ got gos - pel in the air, _

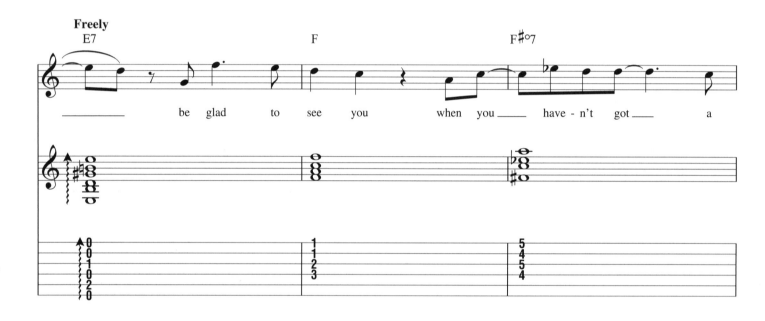

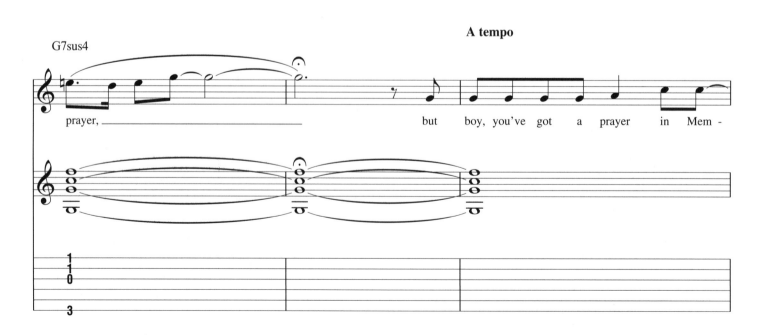

-phis.

D.S. al Coda

Am

3. Now

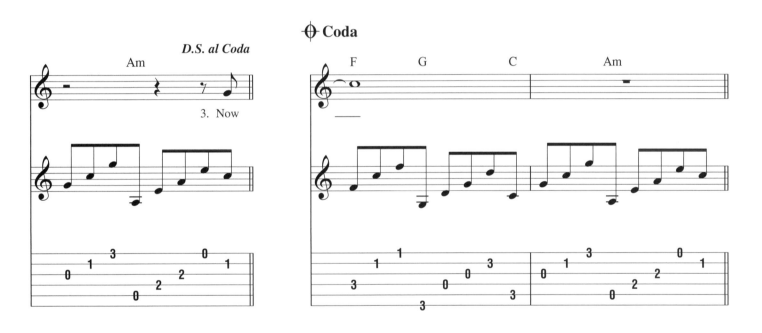

Coda

F   G   C   Am

113

A Whiter Shade of Pale

Words and Music by Keith Reid, Gary Brooker and Matthew Fisher

© Copyright 1967 (Renewed) Onward Music Ltd., London, England
TRO - Essex Music, Inc., New York, controls all publication rights for the U.S.A. and Canada
International Copyright Secured
All Rights Reserved Including Public Performance For Profit
Used by Permission

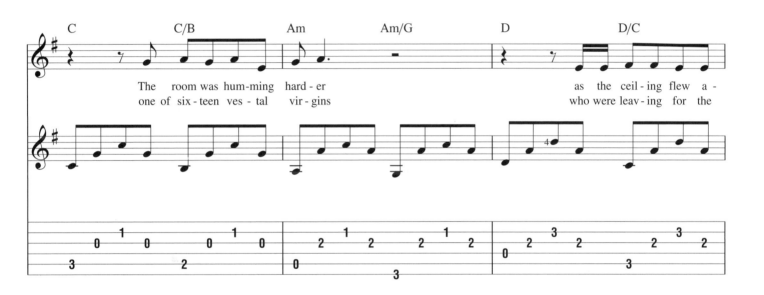

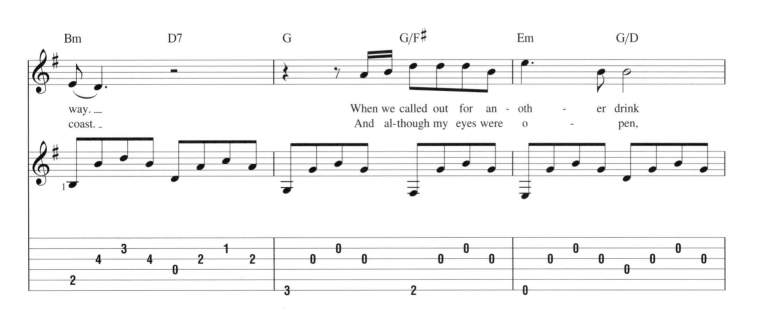

Wonderful Tonight

Words and Music by Eric Clapton

1. It's late in the eve - ning.
2. We go to a par - ty
3. It's time to go home ___ now

She's won-d'ring what clothes ___
and ev - 'ry - one turns ___
and I've got an ach - ing

Copyright © 1977 by Eric Patrick Clapton
Copyright Renewed
All Rights in the U.S. Administered by Unichappell Music Inc.
International Copyright Secured   All Rights Reserved

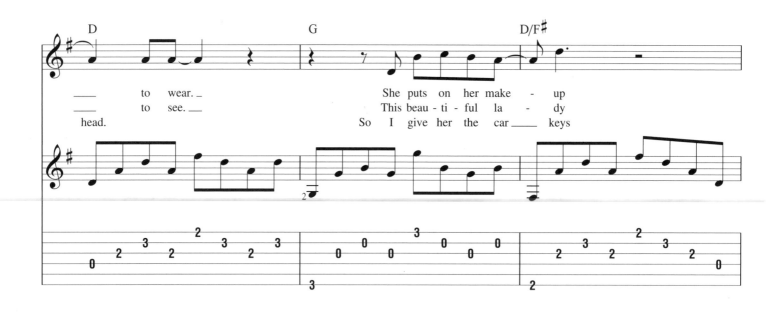

118

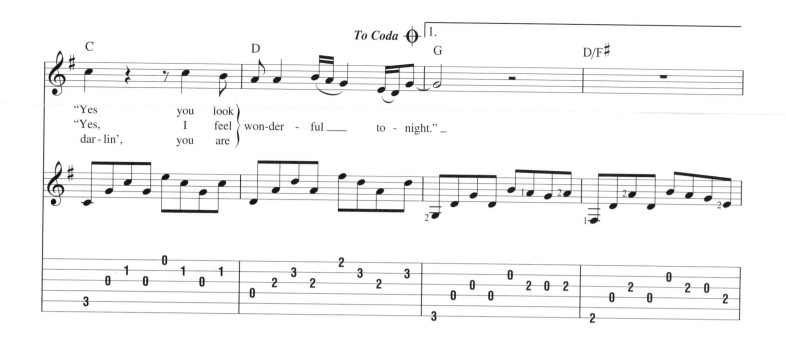

won-der   of it all ___   is that you just don't re - al - ize ___ how much _ I love _

Interlude

___ you.

D.S. al Coda

Coda

Oh my dar-lin', you are won-der-ful ___ to - night. ___

Outro

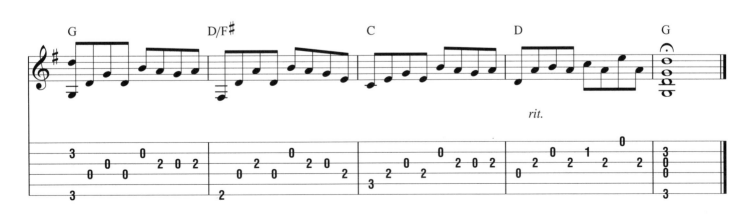

rit.

You Are So Beautiful

Words and Music by Billy Preston and Bruce Fisher

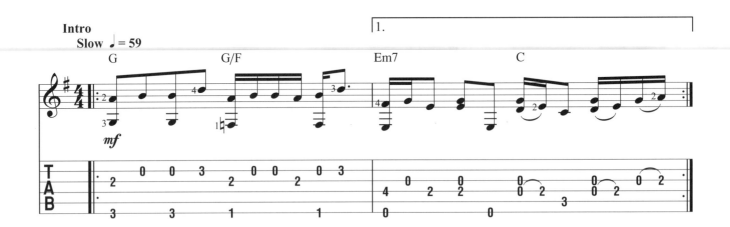

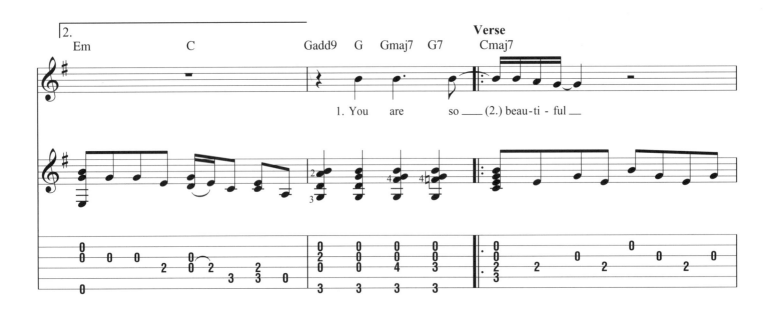

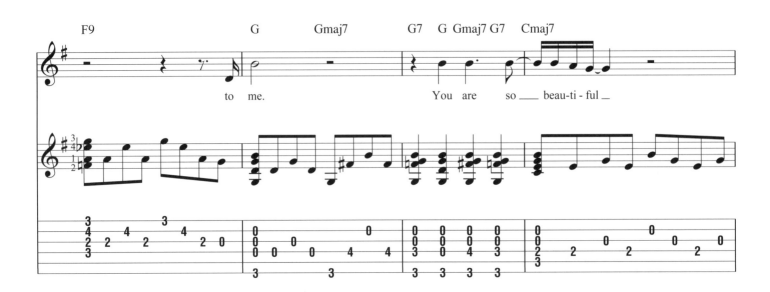

Copyright © 1973 IRVING MUSIC, INC. and ALMO MUSIC CORP.
Copyright Renewed
All Rights Reserved   Used by Permission

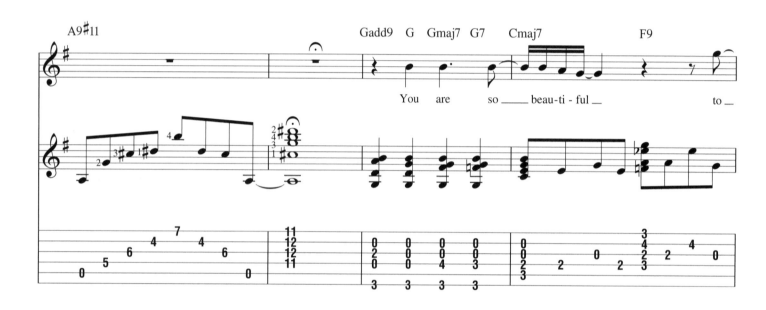

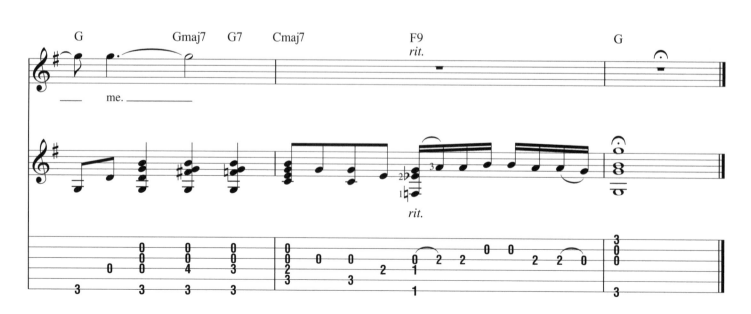

124

You're the Inspiration

Words and Music by Peter Cetera and David Foster

Capo VI

Intro

Slow ♩ = 73

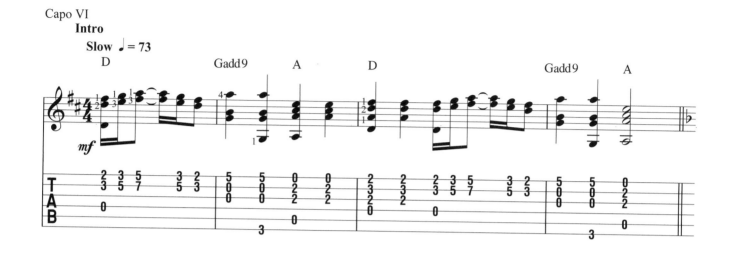

Verse

1. You know our love was meant to be _____
(2.) know, (Yes, I know.) yes, I know that it's plain to see _____

the kind of love _____ that lasts _____ for-ev-er. _____
we're so in love _____ when we're _ to-geth-er. _____

Now I

Copyright © 1984 by Universal Music - MGB Songs and Peermusic III, Ltd.
International Copyright Secured   All Rights Reserved

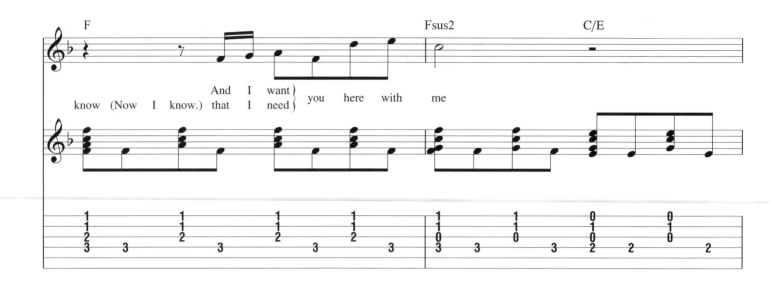

know (Now I know.) that I need you here with me

from to-night ___ un-til the end ___ of time.

Pre-Chorus

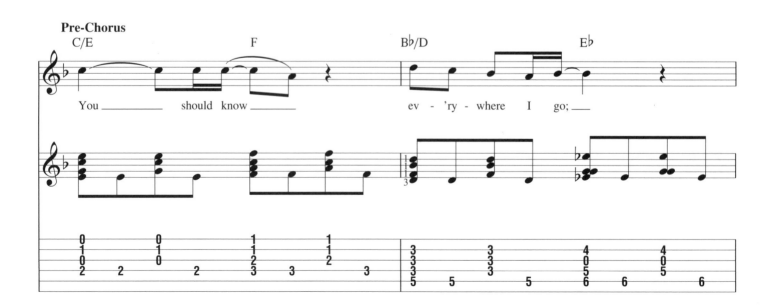

You ___ should know ___ ev-'ry-where I go; ___

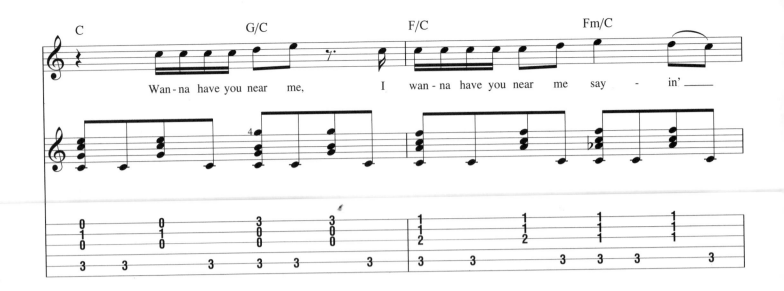

Wan-na have you near me, I wan-na have you near me say - in' _____

no one needs you more _ than I _____ need you.

2. And I no one needs you more than

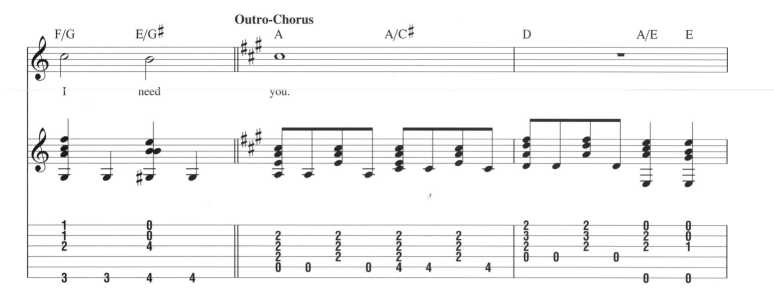

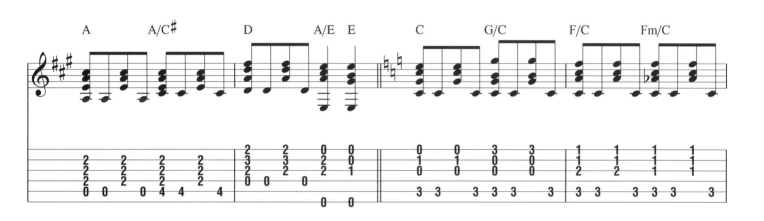

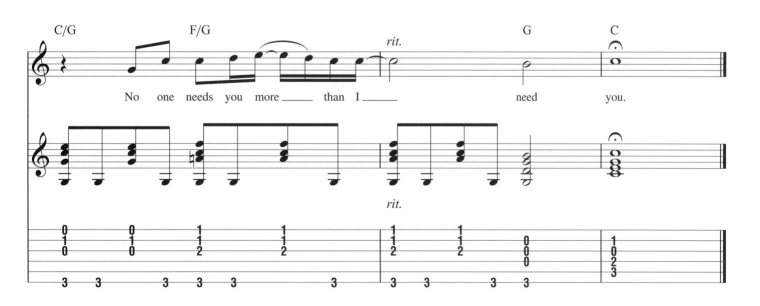

You Raise Me Up

Words and Music by Brendan Graham and Rolf Lovland

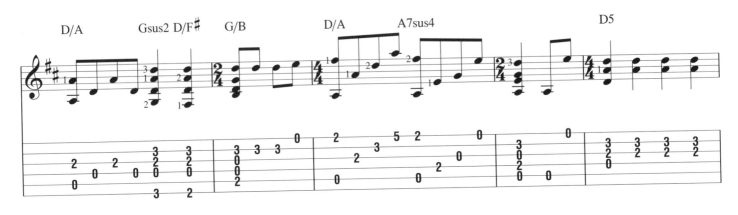

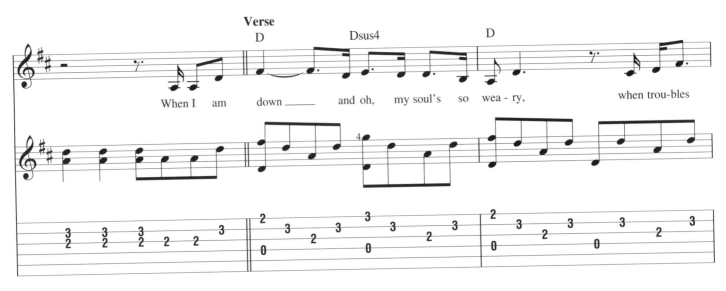

Copyright © 2002 by Peermusic (UK) Ltd. and Universal Music Publishing, A Division of Universal Music AS
All Rights for Peermusic (UK) Ltd. in the United States Controlled and Administered by Peermusic III, Ltd.
All Rights for Universal Music Publishing, A Division of Universal Music AS in the United States and Canada Controlled and Administered by
Universal - PolyGram International Publishing, Inc. (Publishing) and Alfred Music (Print)
International Copyright Secured   All Rights Reserved

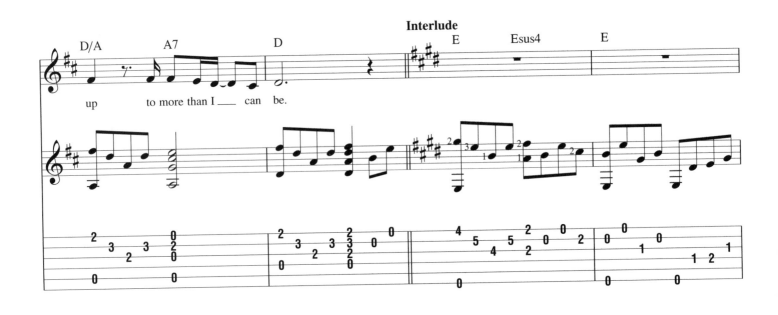

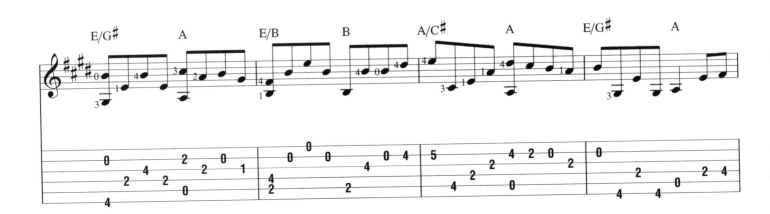

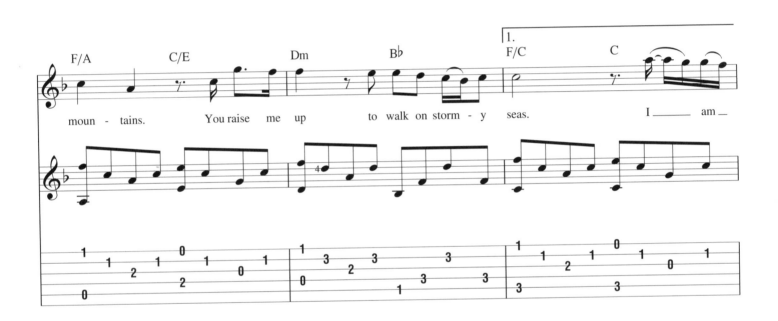

134

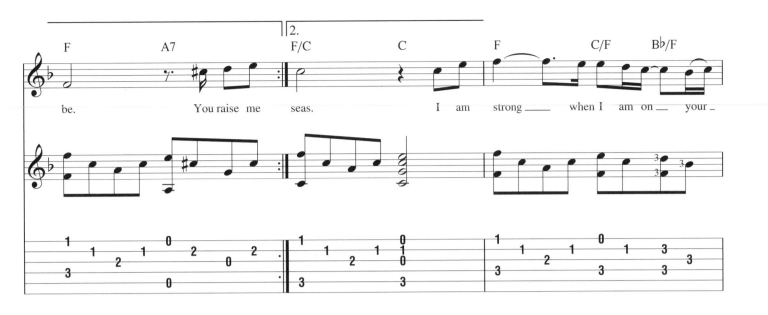

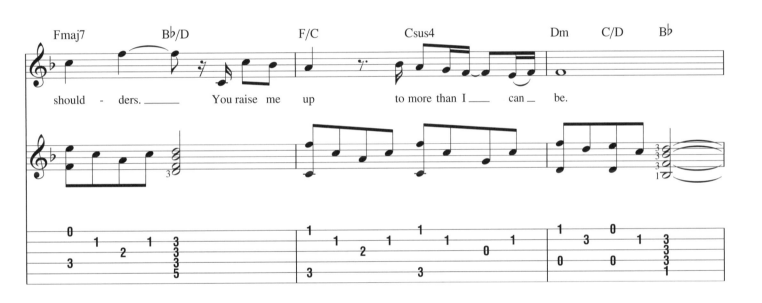

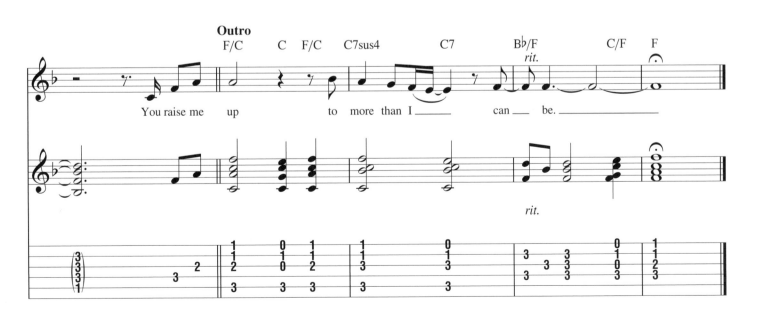

Your Song

Words and Music by Elton John and Bernie Taupin

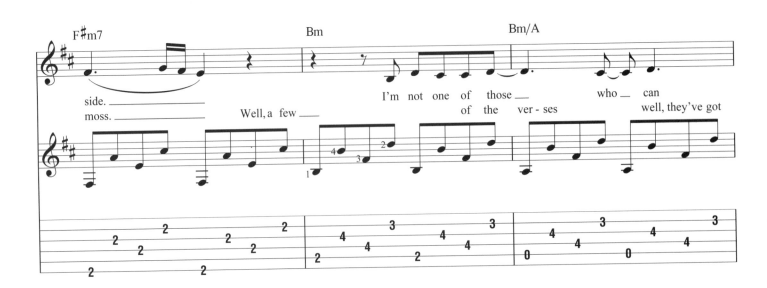

Copyright © 1969 UNIVERSAL/DICK JAMES MUSIC LTD.
Copyright Renewed
All Rights in the United States and Canada Controlled and Administered by
UNIVERSAL - SONGS OF POLYGRAM INTERNATIONAL, INC.
All Rights Reserved   Used by Permission

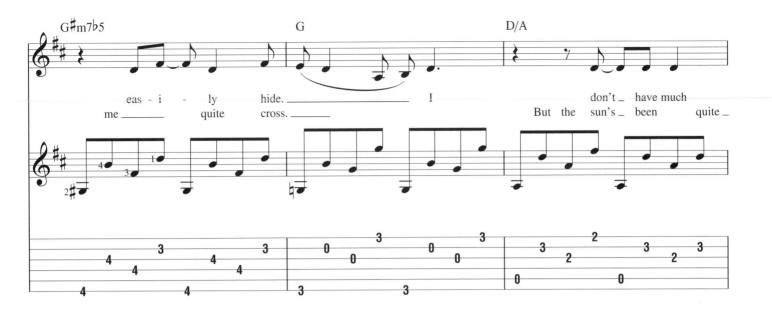

137

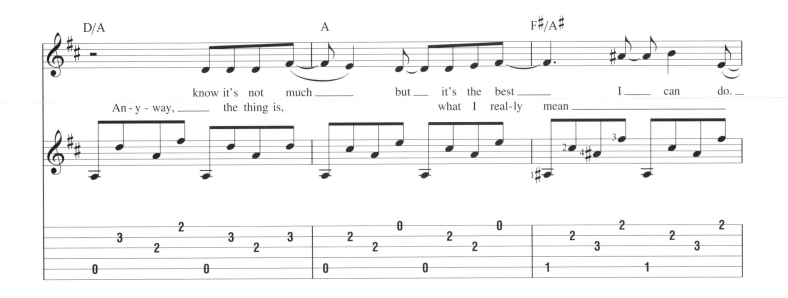

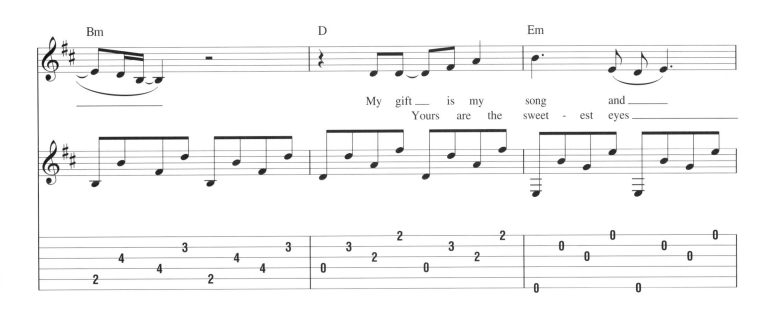

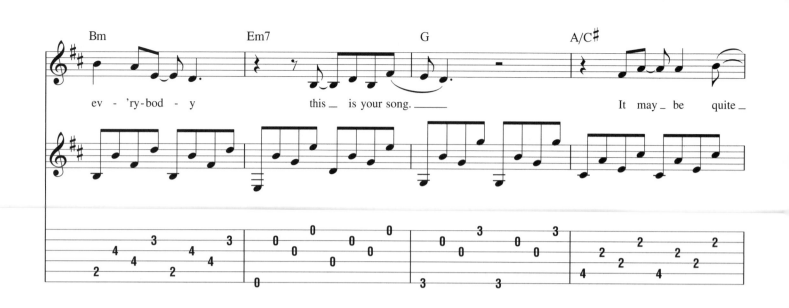

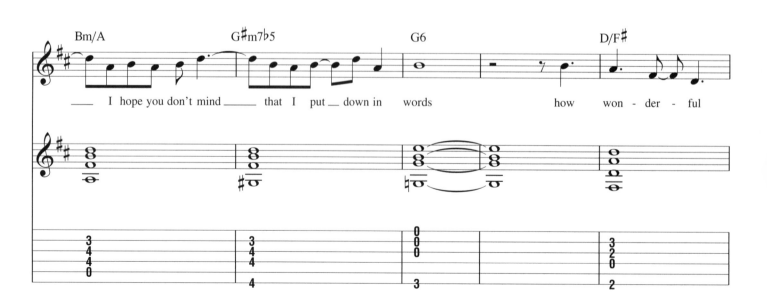

FINGERPICKING GUITAR BOOKS

Hone your fingerpicking skills with these great songbooks featuring solo guitar arrangements in standard notation and tablature. The arrangements in these books are carefully written for intermediate-level guitarists. Each song combines melody and harmony in one superb guitar fingerpicking arrangement. Each book also includes an introduction to basic fingerstyle guitar.

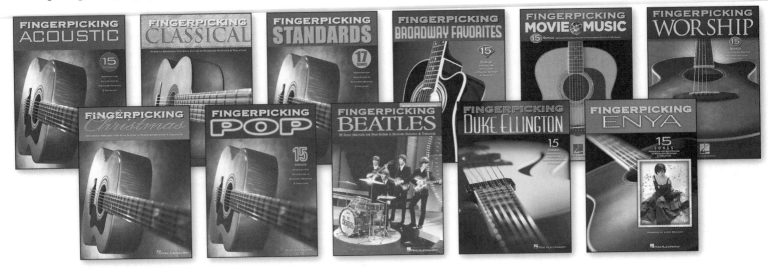

FINGERPICKING ACOUSTIC
00699614......................................$10.99

FINGERPICKING ACOUSTIC ROCK
00699764......................................$9.99

FINGERPICKING BACH
00699793......................................$8.95

FINGERPICKING BALLADS
00699717......................................$9.99

FINGERPICKING BEATLES
00699049......................................$19.99

FINGERPICKING BEETHOVEN
00702390......................................$7.99

FINGERPICKING BLUES
00701277 ....$7.99

FINGERPICKING BROADWAY FAVORITES
00699843......................................$9.99

FINGERPICKING BROADWAY HITS
00699838......................................$7.99

FINGERPICKING CELTIC FOLK
00701148......................................$7.99

FINGERPICKING CHILDREN'S SONGS
00699712......................................$9.99

FINGERPICKING CHRISTIAN
00701076 ....$7.99

FINGERPICKING CHRISTMAS
00699599......................................$8.95

FINGERPICKING CHRISTMAS CLASSICS
00701695......................................$7.99

FINGERPICKING CLASSICAL
00699620......................................$8.95

FINGERPICKING COUNTRY
00699687......................................$9.99

FINGERPICKING DISNEY
00699711......................................$10.99

FINGERPICKING DUKE ELLINGTON
00699845......................................$9.99

FINGERPICKING ENYA
00701161......................................$9.99

FINGERPICKING GOSPEL
00701059......................................$7.99

FINGERPICKING GUITAR BIBLE
00691040 ....$19.99

FINGERPICKING HYMNS
00699688......................................$8.95

FINGERPICKING IRISH SONGS
00701965......................................$7.99

FINGERPICKING JAZZ STANDARDS
00699840......................................$7.99

FINGERPICKING LATIN STANDARDS
00699837......................................$7.99

FINGERPICKING ANDREW LLOYD WEBBER
00699839......................................$9.99

FINGERPICKING LOVE SONGS
00699841......................................$9.99

FINGERPICKING LOVE STANDARDS
00699836 ....$9.99

FINGERPICKING LULLABYES
00701276......................................$9.99

FINGERPICKING MOVIE MUSIC
00699919......................................$9.99

FINGERPICKING MOZART
00699794......................................$8.95

FINGERPICKING POP
00699615......................................$9.99

FINGERPICKING PRAISE
00699714......................................$8.95

FINGERPICKING ROCK
00699716......................................$9.99

FINGERPICKING STANDARDS
00699613......................................$9.99

FINGERPICKING WEDDING
00699637......................................$9.99

FINGERPICKING WORSHIP
00700554......................................$7.99

FINGERPICKING NEIL YOUNG – GREATEST HITS
00700134......................................$12.99

FINGERPICKING YULETIDE
00699654......................................$9.99

HAL•LEONARD® CORPORATION
7777 W. BLUEMOUND RD. P.O. BOX 13819 MILWAUKEE, WI 53213

Visit Hal Leonard online at **www.halleonard.com**

Prices, contents and availability subject to change without notice.

0113

AUTHENTIC CHORDS · ORIGINAL KEYS · COMPLETE SONGS

The *Strum It* series lets players strum the chords and sing along with their favorite hits. Each song has been selected because it can be played with regular open chords, barre chords, or other moveable chord types. Guitarists can simply play the rhythm, or play and sing along through the entire song. All songs are shown in their original keys complete with chords, strum patterns, melody and lyrics. Wherever possible, the chord voicings from the recorded versions are notated.

THE BEACH BOYS' GREATEST HITS
_____00699357............................. $12.95

THE BEATLES FAVORITES
_____00699249............................. $14.95

BEST OF CONTEMPORARY CHRISTIAN
_____00699531............................. $12.95

BEST OF STEVEN CURTIS CHAPMAN
_____00699530............................. $12.95

VERY BEST OF JOHNNY CASH
_____00699514............................. $14.99

CELTIC GUITAR SONGBOOK
_____00699265............................. $9.95

CHRISTMAS SONGS FOR GUITAR
_____00699247............................. $10.95

CHRISTMAS SONGS WITH 3 CHORDS
_____00699487............................. $8.95

VERY BEST OF ERIC CLAPTON
_____00699560............................. $12.95

COUNTRY STRUMMIN'
_____00699119............................. $8.95

JIM CROCE – CLASSIC HITS
_____00699269............................. $10.95

VERY BEST OF JOHN DENVER
_____00699488............................. $12.95

NEIL DIAMOND
_____00699593............................. $12.95

DISNEY FAVORITES
_____00699171............................. $10.95

BEST OF THE DOORS
_____00699177............................. $12.99

MELISSA ETHERIDGE GREATEST HITS
_____00699518............................. $12.99

FAVORITE SONGS WITH 3 CHORDS
_____00699112............................. $8.95

FAVORITE SONGS WITH 4 CHORDS
_____00699270............................. $8.95

FIRESIDE SING-ALONG
_____00699273............................. $8.95

FOLK FAVORITES
_____00699517............................. $8.95

IRVING BERLIN'S GOD BLESS AMERICA®
_____00699508............................. $9.95

GREAT '50s ROCK
_____00699187............................. $9.95

GREAT '60s ROCK
_____00699188............................. $9.95

GREAT '70s ROCK
_____00699262............................. $9.95

**THE GUITAR STRUMMERS'
ROCK SONGBOOK**
_____00701678............................. $14.99

BEST OF WOODY GUTHRIE
_____00699496............................. $12.95

JOHN HIATT COLLECTION
_____00699398............................. $12.95

THE VERY BEST OF BOB MARLEY
_____00699524............................. $12.95

A MERRY CHRISTMAS SONGBOOK
_____00699211............................. $9.95

MORE FAVORITE SONGS WITH 3 CHORDS
_____00699532............................. $8.95

THE VERY BEST OF TOM PETTY
_____00699336............................. $12.95

POP-ROCK GUITAR FAVORITES
_____00699088............................. $8.95

ELVIS! GREATEST HITS
_____00699276............................. $10.95

BEST OF GEORGE STRAIT
_____00699235............................. $14.99

TAYLOR SWIFT FOR ACOUSTIC GUITAR
_____00109717............................. $16.99

BEST OF HANK WILLIAMS JR.
_____00699224............................. $12.95

HAL•LEONARD®
7777 W. Bluemound Rd. P.O. Box 13819 Milwaukee, WI 53213

Visit Hal Leonard online at **www.halleonard.com**

Prices, contents & availability subject to
change without notice.

0113

HAL•LEONARD GUITAR PLAY•ALONG

This series will help you play your favorite songs quickly and easily. Just follow the tab and listen to the CD to the hear how the guitar should sound, and then play along using the separate backing tracks. Mac or PC users can also slow down the tempo without changing pitch by using the CD in their computer. The melody and lyrics are included in the book so that you can sing or simply follow along.

 INCLUDES TAB

VOL. 1 – ROCK	00699570 / $16.99	
VOL. 2 – ACOUSTIC	00699569 / $16.95	
VOL. 3 – HARD ROCK	00699573 / $16.95	
VOL. 4 – POP/ROCK	00699571 / $16.99	
VOL. 5 – MODERN ROCK	00699574 / $16.99	
VOL. 6 – '90s ROCK	00699572 / $16.99	
VOL. 7 – BLUES	00699575 / $16.95	
VOL. 8 – ROCK	00699585 / $14.99	
VOL. 9 – PUNK ROCK	00699576 / $14.95	
VOL. 10 – ACOUSTIC	00699586 / $16.95	
VOL. 11 – EARLY ROCK	00699579 / $14.95	
VOL. 12 – POP/ROCK	00699587 / $14.95	
VOL. 13 – FOLK ROCK	00699581 / $15.99	
VOL. 14 – BLUES ROCK	00699582 / $16.95	
VOL. 15 – R&B	00699583 / $14.95	
VOL. 16 – JAZZ	00699584 / $15.95	
VOL. 17 – COUNTRY	00699588 / $15.95	
VOL. 18 – ACOUSTIC ROCK	00699577 / $15.95	
VOL. 19 – SOUL	00699578 / $14.99	
VOL. 20 – ROCKABILLY	00699580 / $14.95	
VOL. 21 – YULETIDE	00699602 / $14.95	
VOL. 22 – CHRISTMAS	00699600 / $15.95	
VOL. 23 – SURF	00699635 / $14.95	
VOL. 24 – ERIC CLAPTON	00699649 / $17.99	
VOL. 25 – LENNON & McCARTNEY	00699642 / $16.99	
VOL. 26 – ELVIS PRESLEY	00699643 / $14.95	
VOL. 27 – DAVID LEE ROTH	00699645 / $16.95	
VOL. 28 – GREG KOCH	00699646 / $14.95	
VOL. 29 – BOB SEGER	00699647 / $15.99	
VOL. 30 – KISS	00699644 / $16.99	
VOL. 31 – CHRISTMAS HITS	00699652 / $14.95	
VOL. 32 – THE OFFSPRING	00699653 / $14.95	
VOL. 33 – ACOUSTIC CLASSICS	00699656 / $16.95	
VOL. 34 – CLASSIC ROCK	00699658 / $16.95	
VOL. 35 – HAIR METAL	00699660 / $16.95	
VOL. 36 – SOUTHERN ROCK	00699661 / $16.95	
VOL. 37 – ACOUSTIC METAL	00699662 / $16.95	
VOL. 38 – BLUES	00699663 / $16.95	
VOL. 39 – '80s METAL	00699664 / $16.99	
VOL. 40 – INCUBUS	00699668 / $17.95	
VOL. 41 – ERIC CLAPTON	00699669 / $16.95	
VOL. 42 – 2000s ROCK	00699670 / $16.99	
VOL. 43 – LYNYRD SKYNYRD	00699681 / $17.95	
VOL. 44 – JAZZ	00699689 / $14.99	
VOL. 45 – TV THEMES	00699718 / $14.95	
VOL. 46 – MAINSTREAM ROCK	00699722 / $16.95	
VOL. 47 – HENDRIX SMASH HITS	00699723 / $19.95	
VOL. 48 – AEROSMITH CLASSICS	00699724 / $17.99	
VOL. 49 – STEVIE RAY VAUGHAN	00699725 / $17.99	
VOL. 51 – ALTERNATIVE '90s	00699727 / $14.99	
VOL. 52 – FUNK	00699728 / $14.95	

VOL. 53 – DISCO	00699729 / $14.99	
VOL. 54 – HEAVY METAL	00699730 / $14.95	
VOL. 55 – POP METAL	00699731 / $14.95	
VOL. 56 – FOO FIGHTERS	00699749 / $15.99	
VOL. 57 – SYSTEM OF A DOWN	00699751 / $14.95	
VOL. 58 – BLINK-182	00699772 / $14.95	
VOL. 60 – 3 DOORS DOWN	00699774 / $14.95	
VOL. 61 – SLIPKNOT	00699775 / $16.99	
VOL. 62 – CHRISTMAS CAROLS	00699798 / $12.95	
VOL. 63 – CREEDENCE CLEARWATER REVIVAL	00699802 / $16.99	
VOL. 64 – THE ULTIMATE OZZY OSBOURNE	00699803 / $16.99	
VOL. 65 – THE DOORS	00699806 / $16.99	
VOL. 66 – THE ROLLING STONES	00699807 / $16.95	
VOL. 67 – BLACK SABBATH	00699808 / $16.99	
VOL. 68 – PINK FLOYD – DARK SIDE OF THE MOON	00699809 / $16.99	
VOL. 69 – ACOUSTIC FAVORITES	00699810 / $14.95	
VOL. 70 – OZZY OSBOURNE	00699805 / $16.99	
VOL. 71 – CHRISTIAN ROCK	00699824 / $14.95	
VOL. 72 – ACOUSTIC '90s	00699827 / $14.95	
VOL. 73 – BLUESY ROCK	00699829 / $16.99	
VOL. 74 – PAUL BALOCHE	00699831 / $14.95	
VOL. 75 – TOM PETTY	00699882 / $16.99	
VOL. 76 – COUNTRY HITS	00699884 / $14.95	
VOL. 77 – BLUEGRASS	00699910 / $14.99	
VOL. 78 – NIRVANA	00700132 / $16.99	
VOL. 79 – NEIL YOUNG	00700133 / $24.99	
VOL. 80 – ACOUSTIC ANTHOLOGY	00700175 / $19.95	
VOL. 81 – ROCK ANTHOLOGY	00700176 / $22.99	
VOL. 82 – EASY SONGS	00700177 / $12.99	
VOL. 83 – THREE CHORD SONGS	00700178 / $16.99	
VOL. 84 – STEELY DAN	00700200 / $16.99	
VOL. 85 – THE POLICE	00700269 / $16.99	
VOL. 86 – BOSTON	00700465 / $16.99	
VOL. 87 – ACOUSTIC WOMEN	00700763 / $14.99	
VOL. 88 – GRUNGE	00700467 / $16.99	
VOL. 90 – CLASSICAL POP	00700469 / $14.99	
VOL. 91 – BLUES INSTRUMENTALS	00700505 / $14.99	
VOL. 92 – EARLY ROCK INSTRUMENTALS	00700506 / $14.99	
VOL. 93 – ROCK INSTRUMENTALS	00700507 / $16.99	
VOL. 95 – BLUES CLASSICS	00700509 / $14.99	
VOL. 96 – THIRD DAY	00700560 / $14.95	
VOL. 97 – ROCK BAND	00700703 / $14.99	
VOL. 98 – ROCK BAND	00700704 / $14.95	
VOL. 99 – ZZ TOP	00700762 / $16.99	
VOL. 100 – B.B. KING	00700466 / $16.99	
VOL. 101 – SONGS FOR BEGINNERS	00701917 / $14.99	
VOL. 102 – CLASSIC PUNK	00700769 / $14.99	
VOL. 103 – SWITCHFOOT	00700773 / $16.99	

VOL. 104 – DUANE ALLMAN	00700846 / $16.99	
VOL. 106 – WEEZER	00700958 / $14.99	
VOL. 107 – CREAM	00701069 / $16.99	
VOL. 108 – THE WHO	00701053 / $16.99	
VOL. 109 – STEVE MILLER	00701054 / $14.99	
VOL. 111 – JOHN MELLENCAMP	00701056 / $14.99	
VOL. 112 – QUEEN	00701052 / $16.99	
VOL. 113 – JIM CROCE	00701058 / $15.99	
VOL. 114 – BON JOVI	00701060 / $14.99	
VOL. 115 – JOHNNY CASH	00701070 / $16.99	
VOL. 116 – THE VENTURES	00701124 / $14.99	
VOL. 118 – ERIC JOHNSON	00701353 / $14.99	
VOL. 119 – AC/DC CLASSICS	00701356 / $17.99	
VOL. 120 – PROGRESSIVE ROCK	00701457 / $14.99	
VOL. 121 – U2	00701508 / $16.99	
VOL. 123 – LENNON & McCARTNEY ACOUSTIC	00701614 / $16.99	
VOL. 124 – MODERN WORSHIP	00701629 / $14.99	
VOL. 125 – JEFF BECK	00701687 / $16.99	
VOL. 126 – BOB MARLEY	00701701 / $16.99	
VOL. 127 – 1970s ROCK	00701739 / $14.99	
VOL. 128 – 1960s ROCK	00701740 / $14.99	
VOL. 129 – MEGADETH	00701741 / $16.99	
VOL. 131 – 1990s ROCK	00701743 / $14.99	
VOL. 132 – COUNTRY ROCK	00701757 / $15.99	
VOL. 133 – TAYLOR SWIFT	00701894 / $16.99	
VOL. 134 – AVENGED SEVENFOLD	00701906 / $16.99	
VOL. 136 – GUITAR THEMES	00701922 / $14.99	
VOL. 138 – BLUEGRASS CLASSICS	00701967 / $14.99	
VOL. 139 – GARY MOORE	00702370 / $16.99	
VOL. 140 – MORE STEVIE RAY VAUGHAN	00702396 / $17.99	
VOL. 141 – ACOUSTIC HITS	00702401 / $16.99	
VOL. 142 – KINGS OF LEON	00702418 / $16.99	
VOL. 144 – DJANGO REINHARDT	00702531 / $16.99	
VOL. 145 – DEF LEPPARD	00702532 / $16.99	
VOL. 147 – SIMON & GARFUNKEL	14041591 / $16.99	
VOL. 149 – AC/DC HITS	14041593 / $17.99	
VOL. 150 – ZAKK WYLDE	02501717 / $16.99	
VOL. 153 – RED HOT CHILI PEPPERS	00702990 / $19.99	
VOL. 157 – FLEETWOOD MAC	00101382 / $16.99	
VOL. 158 – ULTIMATE CHRISTMAS	00101889 / $14.99	
VOL. 161 – THE EAGLES – ACOUSTIC	00102659 / $16.99	
VOL. 162 – THE EAGLES HITS	00102667 / $17.99	
VOL. 166 – MODERN BLUES	00700764 / $16.99	

Complete song lists available online.

Prices, contents, and availability subject to change without notice.

HAL•LEONARD® CORPORATION
7777 W. BLUEMOUND RD. P.O. BOX 13819 MILWAUKEE, WI 53213
www.halleonard.com

0113